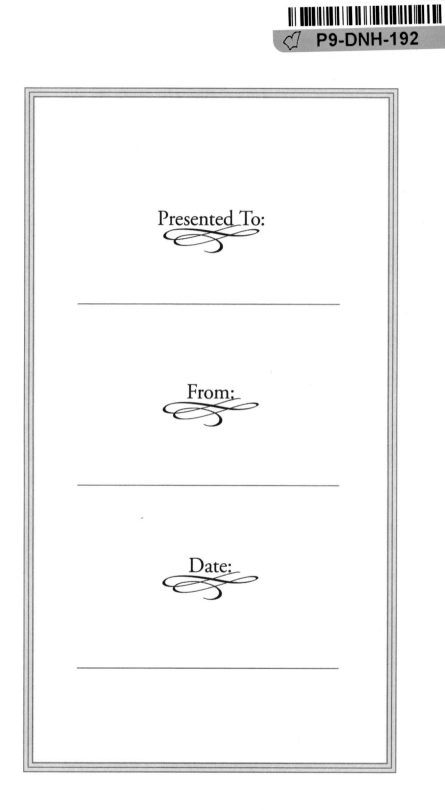

Presented To:

_____

From:

_____

Date:

_____

EYES
OF
HONOR

BOOKS BY JONATHAN WELTON

The School of the Seers

Normal Christianity

Raptureless

AVAILABLE FROM DESTINY IMAGE PUBLISHERS

EYES
OF
HONOR

Training for Purity & Righteousness

JONATHAN WELTON

DESTINY IMAGE® PUBLISHERS, INC.

P.O. Box 310, Shippensburg, PA 17257-0310

"Promoting Inspired Lives."

This book and all other Destiny Image, Revival Press, MercyPlace, Fresh Bread, Destiny Image Fiction, and Treasure House books are available at Christian bookstores and distributors worldwide.

For a U.S. bookstore nearest you, call 1-800-722-6774.

For more information on foreign distributors, call 717-532-3040.

Reach us on the Internet: www.destinyimage.com.

ISBN 13 TP: 978-0-7684-4132-1

ISBN 13 Ebook: 978-0-7684-8829-6

For Worldwide Distribution, Printed in the U.S.A.

1 2 3 4 5 6 7 8 / 16 15 14 13 12

ENDORSEMENTS

Jonathan Welton is one of my heroes. He takes on challenging themes with courage and creativity. I always learn from him. This book is stunningly profound. He got my attention and kept it. This is not a simplistic approach to a topic that impacts virtually all Christian men. Those who read this book will find themselves deeply impacted. As one (with most men) who struggles with sexual purity, I am grateful that Jonathan chose to address this theme and offer solid answers.

DR. JOHN RODDAM
President of Pleroma International
Former Rector of St. Luke's Episcopal, Seattle, WA

This incredible book empowers men to become true protectors and rescuers of women and look upon them with eyes of honor. I highly recommend this book for men who want true change in their lives. Jonathan Welton is not only a powerhouse writer but a true man.

SHELLEY LUBBEN
President of Pink Cross Foundation
Former porn star

Jonathan has something to say. This is not a rehashing of old methods. Jonathan has revelation. When you start reading, you first wonder if it is true. Then you continue reading and begin to hope that it is true. Then you submerge yourself in the message and you know it is true. God is speaking through Jonathan's words. Listen and you will find freedom.

HAROLD EBERLE
President of Worldcast Ministries and Publishing

Jonathan has written one of the best books on being free from bondage by dealing with the root issues of sin. I highly recommend reading this book, and you should be prepared to receive your breakthrough.

DR. CHÉ AHN
Senior Pastor, HROCK Church, Pasadena, CA
President, Harvest International Ministry
International Chancellor, Wagner Leadership Institute

Finally, a book that doesn't just deal with the fruit of the problem, but the root of overcoming the lie of men's identity. Jonathan Welton gives you raw truth about a national problem that we've shoved under the carpet for far too long; the addiction to pornography and the sexualization of women. It offers not only total freedom, but practical steps to facing the problem head on. This book has the capacity to not only change our churches, but our culture—restoring the identity of men and giving them *Eyes of Honor*.

ANNY DONEWALD
Founder, Eve's Angels Inc.
Former stripper and call girl

Jonathan Welton has addressed a pressing need in the lives of many men in the Body of Christ. Sharing from his own struggles and his many attempts to find freedom will surely encourage men who long for purity and freedom from any type of sexual addiction. Jonathan found keys that resulted in lasting freedom and shares the truths that set him free. May this book start a fire of purity that spreads through the Body of Christ and releases many from the chains of bondage.

Joe McIntyre
President, International Fellowship of Ministries

Jonathan Welton has found the cure to the common cold. Welton's biblical and practical approach to sexual purity does not involve cold showers, shock collars, or faith-based spyware. Welton instead approaches the topic from a refreshingly new point of view. *Eyes of Honor* is not a dude book, it's an identity book for a multigender, multigenerational audience.

Darren Stott
Lead Pastor, The Seattle Revival Center

Herein Jonathan deals with one of the key issues for all Christians. How do you really overcome the power of the evil one? How do you triumph over the lusts of the flesh? Jonathan shows that our Lord provides the answer to the lusts of the flesh. With God all things are possible. Here is an ideal chance to show that through Christ all is possible. Read this book and move from despair to triumph by putting into practice the victory that has already been won.

The Reverend Canon Dr. Andrew P.B. White
Vicar of Baghdad
Director of the High Council of Religious Leaders in Iraq

I have discovered that Jonathan Welton is a prophetic voice for our generation. In his book, *The Eyes of Honor*, Jonathan has given fresh insight and tools for living a life of purity. I have had the opportunity to personally observe many ministers display the power of God who have great influence in the Body of Christ. I always enjoy watching the manifestation of the power of God displayed through someone's gifting, but it has been my experience that a person's character needs to match the level of their gifting. Gifting will bring platforms of influence, but character will keep you there safely.

I believe that *Eyes of Honor* will set you on a path of personal freedom, further propelling you into your destiny, releasing Heaven on Earth. I would greatly encourage you to read this timely book.

CHAD DEDMON,
Co-Author of *Risk Factor,*
International Speaker, Encountering Jesus Ministries

Eyes of Honor will open your eyes and heart to fresh revelations of God's love and presence. I commend his insightful book as a guide to deeper intimacy with the Spirit and a map for your spiritual journey. Once we grasp the revelation of the Gospel, that we truly have been crucified with Christ and have died to our old nature, life blossoms, sin repulses us, and Kingdom life brings exhilaration and deep intimacy with Christ and others.

DR. ALAN N. KEIRAN
Captain, Chaplain Corps, USN (Ret)
Chief of Staff, U.S. Senate Chaplain's Office
Washington, DC

Eyes of Honor has addressed the challenge of addiction of any kind with biblical clarity, courage, and great hope. Jonathan's emphasis on a necessary change of focus—not to victory but from victory, not predators but protectors, not in bondage but in freedom—are powerful keys to right-mindedness and right living. The "but rather" and other tools he provides are practical, powerful, and effective. This is a book I can highly recommend to my own clients. The contents of this book will empower not just individuals, but communities to rise up and rescue the lost and broken!

PATRICIA BYERS MS, NCP, LMHC
Mental Health Therapist, Yakima, WA
Advisory Board, Healing & Training Center of Yakima

The largest contributing factor to morality struggles among Christians is the Church's obsession with moralizing. We were never tasked to moralize the world, but rather to preach the scandal of grace. This book is refreshing in that it points neither to external nor internal exercises at shaping up behavior in a vain attempt to conform men into perfect peaches. Rather, starting from the inside out, Jonathan Welton shows that good behavior is an effortless by-product of recognizing our true identity in Christ. Our perfection has already been completely accomplished in Him. This is the very thing that liberates us to be who we already are. The old is gone; the new has come. As you read this book, let a revelation of the finished work of Christ's cross bring an end to your struggle to be good. Both our addictions and our self-willed attempts to defeat them were crucified with Christ—and now we're simply realizing that we've been woven into a transcendent union life with Godhead.

JOHN CROWDER
Sons of Thunder Ministries & Publications
www.thenewmystics.com

Jonathan Welton is truly ahead of his time and beyond his years with his latest book *Eyes of Honor*. Jonathan represents the voice of a generation that will not minimize the finished work of the cross of Christ. He has taken the battle against sexual sin out of the closet and given a unique understanding about our true identity as new creations in Christ.

JOSH CROFTON
Prophetic Leadership, Mountain Top International
Crofton House Ministries, Yakima, WA

CONTENTS

FOREWORD

by Graham Cook

The cross is the starting point for all of our newness of life. The cross is our crucial point of deliverance from the world, the flesh, and the devil. He who is dead is freed from sin. Jesus did not just die for us, He died as us! We were placed in Him at His crucifixion, His death and burial. Most vitally, we were raised in Him to live an ascended spirituality before God.

God now no longer deals with sin, having accomplished that end in the finished work of Christ. Now He is solely occupied with our righteousness. Every situation provides us with the opportunity to remain in our chosen standing in Christ. We abide in Him. We learn to walk in newness of life. We stay dead! We have permission to consider ourselves dead to sin but alive to God.

In Christ, we are alive to all the possibilities of the Holy Spirit who empowers us to abide in the fullness of God. Eyes of honor must first see Jesus so that we rejoice with power in all that He has accomplished for us, in us, and potentially through us as we joyfully surrender to His love.

We do not become new persons by changing our behavior. We discover the person we already are in Christ and behave accordingly. Eyes of honor are fixed not only on what Jesus has done for us, but also on who He is now in this chapter of our lives. Everything is about training in righteousness, goodness, loving-kindness, grace, mercy, and honor. Every circumstance is concerned with the stance for Christ we are going to take in our lives.

Identity is the echo of belief. It is our identity in Christ that is always being challenged. We are new creations. All the old has passed away and all things have become new. All these things are of God. That means that we are never being challenged by a negative since that is part of the old that has passed away.

If all things are now of God, that surely means that all our challenges in life emanate from His good pleasure. We are not being challenged by the world, the flesh, and the devil. We are being stimulated by Heaven, the Spirit, and the Sovereign Lord. All things may enable us to be made in His image as we learn to abide in Jesus. All things empower us to remain where the Father has placed us—in His beloved Son.

Jonathan's well-written book is about the choices that arise out of abiding. It is about the power of our identity in the true knowledge of Jesus. He is concerned with our inheriting the nature of the Second Adam, not clinging to the shame of the first. We are new creations with the mind of Christ so that we can think as God does about our identity as citizens of Heaven.

I commend Jonathan's book to you. He provides revelation by exegesis and example that will empower you to rise up and overcome every obstacle to a life of honor.

GRAHAM COOKE
Author and Speaker

PREFACE

by Karen Welton

My husband and I have walked down a road that many other couples have walked down, struggling to find solutions to combat the sexual giant of pornography in his life. It is a lonely road filled with tears, deception, and confusion; but if you keep walking, it leads to freedom and victory. I am convinced that if it were not for my husband's unquenchable thirst for truth, we would have ended up defeated on the side of the road, like many couples that have walked this path before us.

When Jonathan hit rock bottom, he found himself confused, scared, and without any answers to help him climb out of the pit. In search for healing, however, he simply refused to accept the mantra that many Christian psychologists and therapists dished up: You are an addict, you are powerless to help yourself, you need accountability, you are depraved, and you are in a never-ending battle with your flesh.

Although, at times, I wished he would just "crucify his flesh," I am so thankful now that he did not accept these lies! Jonathan knew enough to know that this was not the freedom Christ promised us in

His Word. He began a quest to find real answers that would bring lasting freedom. The book you hold in your hands is the blood, sweat, and tears of one man's journey from brokenness to healing and life, and the truths that set him free.

I know these truths work because I saw the transformation with my own eyes: from a scared, cold, and defeated man, to a powerful, vulnerable, and transparent husband. I invite you to experience this same revolution in your own heart. The road ahead is not easy. In fact, it was the hardest thing we have ever walked through in our lives, but the reward of freedom is worth the battle.

If you are ready to take control of your own life, rule over your mind, and open your heart to love again, we invite you on this journey with us. The truths contained herein will counter everything else you have heard from modern clinical therapy, and even popular Christian theology. No matter what addiction you are struggling with, the joy and freedom that Christ purchased for you at the cross is not only available, but obtainable. Today.

We have a choice. We will either believe who satan says we are, or who God says we are. Satan says you are depraved, guilty, and hopeless. God declares you righteous, honorable, and holy in Christ. As a wife, I encourage every woman to give this book to the men in your life. You have the opportunity to declare God's identity over your husbands, brothers, and sons. Then read it yourself and let it set you free from shame, fear, condemnation, as it did me!

It is time to leave fear behind and step into our God-given identities as sons and daughters of God. May you be transformed, strengthened, and inspired by these truths!

In Christ,
KAREN WELTON

INTRODUCTION

Watchman Nee wrote:

From the Holy Scriptures we may see that the life as ordained by God for Christians is one full of joy and rest, one that is uninterrupted communion with God, and is in perfect harmony with His will. It is a life that does not thirst and hunger after the world, that walks outside of sins, and that transcends all things. Indeed, it is a holy, powerful and victorious life, and one that constitutes knowing God's will and having continuous fellowship with Him.

The life which God has ordained for Christians is a life that is hid with Christ in God. Nothing can touch, affect or shake this life. As Christ is unshakable, so we are unshakable. As Christ transcends all things, we also transcend all things. As Christ is before God, so we too are before Him. Let us never entertain the thought that we should be weak and defeated. There is no such thing as weakness and defeat; for "Christ is our life" as declared in Colossians 3.4. He transcends all; He cannot be touched by anything. Hallelujah! This is the life of Christ!

The life ordained for Christians is full of rest, full of joy, full of power, and full of the will of God. But let us inquire of ourselves as to what sort of life we are living today. If our life is not what God has ordained it to be, then we need to know victory. Hence, we shall look into this matter of our experience. And what we shall relate here may not be pleasing to our ears, because some of us are rather pathetic; yet we need to humble ourselves in order that we may see our lack and receive grace from God.[1]

While it may be the experience of the *average* Christian man, it is not *normal* for a Christian man to be plagued emotionally and mentally by sexual temptation. *Average* is defined by what is most common. *Normal* is defined by a standard, and in the Church, Jesus is our standard for normal. Although this struggle against sexual sin has become a common issue in the modern Church, this by no means makes it normal according to the pattern laid out in the New Testament.

When we examine the Word, we find that Christians were expected to live as Jesus did. First John 2:6 says, *"Those who say they live in God should live their lives as Jesus did"* (NLT). History records that the early Church was actually reputed for walking in purity:

In 125 AD, Athenian philosopher Christian Aristides reported on the sexual practices of the Christian church to his king. He said, "They [Christians] do not commit adultery or immorality....Their wives, O king, are as pure as virgins, and their daughters are modest. Their men abstain from all unlawful sexual contact and from impurity, in the hopes of recompense that is to come in another world."[2]

Unfortunately, in the last few decades the Church has fallen into disrepute for its lust and immorality. Yet sexual sin is not exclusively a modern issue. Even classic literature, such as *The Scarlet Letter* by Nathaniel Hawthorne (1850), addressed the issues of sexual temptation and the Christian man.

Though it is not a new issue, over the last 2,000 years of Church history, morality has eroded to the point that sexual sin is considered common in Christian men. This should not be. It is time for the Church to be pure again. We must abandon such low expectations. As Watchman Nee wrote, "May we not deceive ourselves, imagining that sinning is inevitable for a Christian. I think no thought hurts our Lord more than this kind of attitude."[3]

It is time to dig into the roots of sexual sin and find healing for the Christian man. I will start with my story.

PRACTICAL TIPS FOR THIS BOOK

At the end of each chapter you will find *Tools*; these are intended to take the teaching of each chapter and put it into practical use. You will get the most out of this book by actually stopping after each chapter and implementing the *Tool*.

Second, you will notice that this book is divided into three sections. As you will see, my approach to sexual purity is driven by having a correct revelation of our identity in Christ. In Section 1, we cover topics relating to who we are in Christ and how to live in righteous relationships. In Section 2, we look at four areas that commonly seem to be landmines to those pursuing righteous living. Lastly, in Section 3, I take a very different approach to how we should see our sisters around us.

Also, you will notice that the subtitle of this book is *Training for Purity & Righteousness*. This is an important point to grasp. This is not simply a book about sexual purity. Righteousness means to be in right relationship with God *and* with humankind. While I am not intending to write a full-blown relationship book, there are some important topics that should be included in any discussion of sexual purity: such things such as valuing yourself, being a powerful person, resting, and setting boundaries. While I could write purely on lust and only deal with one issue, I would rather write a book about identity, which will teach men to be in right relationship with God and humanity as well as heal the root issues of lust. Actually, the topics in this book can bring health to about 50 different areas, not simply just the issue of lust. Yet because lust is such a big issue, I will keep this in view of the reader at all times.

CHAPTER 1

MY STORY

Growing up, I spent my summers at an all-male Christian summer camp. Hiking, swimming, sports, archery, and horseback riding—this camp had it all. I have calculated that over the years I have spent close to a full year and a half at camp.

Even in this ideal environment, I constantly had young men come and ask for my input regarding how to handle their lustful thoughts. To think that we were completely removed from the presence of females for eight weeks, and yet these young Christian men—and I—still could not separate from the lustful thoughts that filled our minds.

One young man was even caught masturbating in the staff lounge and was sent home. Of course, it is easy to point the finger at how stupid that kid was. But, inside, many of us felt discouraged because the only difference between him and us was that we hid our sin better than he did.

Over the years, I have had hundreds of conversations in which other men have asked me how to deal with lustful thoughts. Even though I grew up with a solid Christian heritage in a homeschooling family, and despite the fact that I earned two masters degrees and won the National Herald of Christ award, I lacked any real answers to offer my friends. I was caught in the same battle as the men who asked my input.

For years I have collected and read books on sexual purity, and yet I have not been satisfied by the answers offered to Christian men. I have heard better advice from my high school friend, Tom, who said, "When I feel tempted, I eat a raw potato. Nothing gets your mind off of naked ladies like eating a raw potato!"

I am not sure that Tom ever actually ate a raw potato, but his idea (though hilarious) is really not that different from the typical advice given to Christian men. Many Christian books try to help men through methods of *behavior modification*. One of the most popular men's purity books of the last decade instructed men to "bounce" their eyes, meaning that one should look away from temptation before lustful thoughts take over.

While this advice might help a little bit, there must be a better answer. The men I have talked to about "bouncing" their eyes eventually found that they could hardly look an attractive woman in the face because of the fear of lusting. The bouncing-eyes approach sounds practical, but it does not reach the roots of lust.

This point was driven home for me while visiting a friend in southern California. We were at a burger joint when the inevitable conversation came up once again. He shared with me, "Jon, I have a beautiful wife, a couple of beautiful children, a wonderful job that provides well for us, a great home, and I couldn't be happier. Yet, I cannot get away from the lust in my eyes; I have talked to dozens of pastors and nobody seems to have answers. I appreciate that other men are honest enough to admit that they don't have answers, but when is someone going to get this figured out?"

At that point, a holy anger arose in my heart and I heard myself say out loud, "How is it that Jesus told us that we can raise the dead but Christian men can't even stop masturbating!" (See Matthew 10:8.)

Perhaps you have tried accountability, online filtering software, men's purity books, attending 12-step groups, or professional counseling, but to no avail. You may be holding this book in your hands wondering if this is going to be another waste of your time, or if, maybe, you have finally stumbled upon a book that has some real answers.

WHAT HASN'T WORKED

I am going to be real with you. This book contains what you need to be free of sexual temptation. I know that this is a big, almost surreal statement, yet I believe it to be true. Before I tell you what makes this book different, I will tell you what I have found in the books that are already on the market.

There are three main categories of books on the market regarding men's purity: 1) books that tell the reader how large the problem of lust is in our society, 2) books that tell a personal story of how the author ruined his whole life by following his lust, and 3) hard-to-read books written by Christian psychologists which describe lust in clinical terms.

There is little variation regarding the approach to this topic. The majority of the books I have read essentially label lust as a disease and leave the Christian man with a weak, carnal answer regarding how to *manage* his disease. But this does not line up with the Word of God; when did Christ ever tell His followers to manage their sin?

May I be honest with you? Because I am writing to men who spend significant amounts of time each week battling lustful thoughts, this is going to be a raw book full of truth and brazenly honest feelings. I am not writing from an ivory tower of perfection. I have had my gut-wrenching battles with temptation, and I have been cut and scarred in the warfare. But I have also come out as a victor. I have found through my personal experience and study of the Word that we can be free. Even though surveys have found that 82 percent of Christian men are privately struggling with lust,[1] it doesn't have to be this way.

The aim of this book is not to put a Band-Aid on the problem; we must get to the roots of the infection. I want to give you hope: there is an antidote. Jesus did not save you from the bondage of 99 percent of your sins just to leave you struggling with lust for the rest of your life. This issue requires delving deeper into the hearts of men in order to finally bring health in this area.

THE ACCOUNTABILITY MYTH

One of the first things I will tell you is that if you must have accountability, then you haven't really found the answer to your sin. Although accountability may help you manage your sin, it doesn't deal with the root. Jesus didn't provide us with complete freedom from the power of sin so that we could establish accountability groups to try not to sin. Jesus didn't have an accountability partner, and neither did the apostles.

I have a high regard for the interdependence of the Body of Christ; yet if we must lean on others *so as not to sin*, there is something fundamentally wrong with our theology. Clearly, the Bible teaches that we are the Body of Christ, and we are many interconnected members (see Rom. 12:5). This does not mean that we must create webs of accountability to keep each other from sinning. That is not taught in the Word.

This is where my approach comes in. I am not a pastor; I am not a counselor; I am not a psychologist. I am a student of the Word. I believe that the Bible has the answer. I also believe that the Bible is not complicated, and that when the Bible is complicated, it is probably being taught wrongly. The Bible is about relationship with God, and He would not want that to be complicated.

I carry a saying with me: *"Wrong teaching leads to wrong living; whereas right teaching leads to right living."* I believe that the struggle for sexual purity comes from wrong teaching. While most Christian men struggling with lust would be happy just to have victory over lust, I believe that the Lord has much more for us.

THE EVIDENCE AGAINST US

Right now the world is suffering from many evils regarding sexual sin. The sex industry worldwide is raking in over $57 billion a year.[2] The sex slave trade is kidnapping, raping, and prostituting our sisters all around the world. Hollywood is ever increasing its degradation of women. Homosexual marriage, sex-change operations, and the abortion agenda are pushing forward in our society every day.

Although Christian leaders oppose these global sins, many continue in personal slavery to pornography, which has the same evil spirits behind it as the rest of these sins. They publically denounce the very spirits of lust and perversion to which they are privately enslaved. How will we ever take down the sex slave industry while we are in bondage to the same evil spirits that are behind it? The Bible's answer is simple:

...if My people, who are called by My name, will humble themselves and pray and seek My face and turn from their wicked ways, then will I hear from heaven, and I will forgive their sin and will heal their land (2 Chronicles 7:14).

The world around us is sin-sick with a toxic poison of lust. The Church must first be healed of this toxicity before we can offer hope, healing, and restoration to a world trapped in sexual bondage. I interpret Second Chronicles 7:14 as saying, *when God's people stop focusing on those around them and deal with their own hearts, then God will bring healing to those around them as well.* God will heal the hearts of the homosexuals, abortionists, pornographers, and the like if, and when, we, as the Church, turn to Him, humble ourselves, and repent of our own sin.

Not only do 82 percent of Christian men regularly struggle with lust, but even those in the pulpit are suffering immensely. As a Church leader, I can say that it is very challenging to find someone safe to share your struggle with. Church leaders carry a heavy burden of expectation on their shoulders, and this makes it even harder to be open about failures and struggles. They fear losing their ministries and callings, so they keep their struggles secret, hoping to beat them on their own. Sadly, many of their stories end tragically. Considering this statistically, many in full-time ministry have been unfaithful to their spouses: "Forty percent of pastors have had extra-marital affairs since entering the ministry."[3]

Those in the pulpit desperately need help too.

If we hope to fix the divorce rate inside the Church, we must find victory against lust. Lust isn't the only thing that causes marriages to fail, but it is almost always a factor. It is not just the sad, depressed, and angry people who are struggling with sexual temptation. "One study of 4,126 male business leaders, executives, and professionals reported that 88% of the men questioned had *at least* one affair."[4]

When we look at the numbers, the problem seems monumental. Yet I believe Jesus has given us a genuine solution that will bring actual freedom to the Church. If we can get freedom from sexual sin inside the Church, then we will begin to have a healing impact on the sin-sick world around us.

THE METHODS I TRIED

On my journey to freedom from sexual bondage, I found that the Church offered many methods for finding freedom. I spent time vigorously trying each of the methods and found limited or temporary freedom. Having exhausted every avenue that I could, I turned to the Lord in my frustration and cried out for true, full, and lasting freedom. I knew that I needed freedom not only for myself, but also for the host of other men struggling in the Body of Christ.

The following are a few of the methods promising freedom that I tried. Perhaps you haven't tried these, and I can forewarn you of certain weaknesses; maybe you are trying these paths and feel like there is more freedom available; or perhaps you have tried them and are discouraged. If you are a part of the third group, be encouraged, because Jesus—the Author and Perfecter of your faith (see Heb. 12:2 NASB)—is going to continue working in your life to bring you to fullness of freedom.

Deliverance From Demonic Oppression

When I first began to feel trapped by pornography, my first thought was that I must be in bondage to a demon of lust. As a Christian, I had heard about demons for many years and thought that I must need deliverance.

I read every book on deliverance that I could find. Here is what I found to be true. The devil is a totally defeated foe and a tremendous liar. After the cross of Christ, the only way the devil can gain power is by getting individuals to agree with his lies. As I began to understand that I had come into agreement with his lies, I worked through deliverance and found a measure of freedom, but I knew there was a greater freedom than what I was experiencing.[5]

Dealing with the Soul

After I realized that I didn't just need a demon cast out of me, I began to look at my emotional life. I was looking for how my life could have become so out of control. I came across the book *The Spiritual Man* by Watchman Nee. Because I had heard so many good things about this book, I hungrily read it, twice in fact!

I began to believe that my lust was a product of my soul not being submitted to my spirit. So I worked as hard as possible to bring my soul into subjection to my spirit. It was many wasted years later that a dear brother showed me the error of this concept. I have devoted a whole chapter to taking apart this myth, but suffice it to say here that *the soul is a good thing that should not be suppressed.* If you have been caught in the "submit your soul to your spirit" teaching, consider reading *Escaping Dualism* by Harold Eberle.

Dualism: The Human Condition

I moved from trying to suppress my soul to instead trying to crucify my fleshly, carnal nature. I began to think that I must "die daily" like the apostle Paul said in his letter to the Corinthians (see 1 Cor. 15:31). Perhaps my problem was my sin nature. I just needed to deny self and pick up my cross. I became focused on my cross and tried to be my own executioner.

After many years of frustration, discouragement, and extensive biblical study, my eyes were opened to this truth: *My crucifixion with Christ is a past-tense, accomplished fact that I can add nothing to.* I cover this in much more detail in a later chapter.

Internet Filters

While a filter may be a helpful preventive tool, it is not a solution. Placing a filter on your mobile phone or computer may help block Internet pornography, but if you must have this, then you have not actually removed the lust from your heart. Internet filters are like childproofing a home; once the child is grown, you do not need to have a childproof home. In the same way, once you have dealt with removing lust from your heart, Internet filters become unnecessary.

Introspection

At this point in my journey, I was not looking for demons, I was not trying to suppress my soul, and I was not trying to crucify myself, so I dug deeper into introspection. I figured that I must begin to "take every thought captive" (see 2 Cor. 10:5). I set a mental guard and filtered my thoughts on a constant basis. It did not take long in this stage for me to begin to feel tired and burnt out. I was working and struggling as hard as I could, but I ended up crying out in my heart like Paul did in Romans 7:24: *"O wretched man that I am! Who will deliver me from this body of death?"* (NKJV).

The Lord began to show me that the focus of introspection was *self.* Knowing that *"the heart is deceitful above all things, and it is exceedingly corrupt..."* (Jer. 17:9 WEB), how could I trust the assessment I gained from my own heart about my own heart!

Introspection was draining my life and getting me nowhere. *I realized that I had placed my focus on myself, rather than turning my focus toward Jesus and His grace.*

Inner Healing

I knew that the Lord was saying that I needed to focus on Him and not myself, but I didn't really know how to do that. And because I was incapable of taking all my thoughts captive, I began to wonder where these thoughts were coming from. I began to look for the roots of my thought life in the experiences and memories that I had accumulated over the years. I did find a new measure of success against lust by working through my memories with repentance and forgiveness.

Unfortunately, I began to feel like I would never reach the bottom of my bucket. I realized that forgiveness and repentance took me from negative 100 back to ground zero; but the Word of God describes a life that is lived at positive 100. Inner healing was very helpful, it helped me deal with the past, but I still didn't have my identity straightened out for walking forward.[6]

The Clinical Approach

Eventually, I sought out Christian counseling with a focus on those caught in sexual bondage. I reasoned that because they work with people with similar issues all the time, then they must have found a way to help people. I submitted to analysis and spent some time in the office of a world-class expert in this arena. I was very excited when I first sat down with him. I thought, "I am in the one place that probably has the answers I have been searching for. I am finally going to find answers!"

Unfortunately, this was the most disappointing point in my journey. Much of modern Christian counseling has been putting Band-Aids on major infections. Having searched and even gone to the top of the sexual purity mountain in search of answers, I was shocked and disappointed to find nothing of the true freedom I sought.

The main three tools incorporated by the clinical approach were completely secular in approach. They are as follows:

Tool 1: Labeling

As I submitted to the professional counselor, I was given a host of labels regarding my bondage to sexual sin. Rather than reinforcing the labels that God has given me—son, beloved, righteous, light of the world, salt of the Earth, royalty, and so forth—the clinical approach placed psychological labels over my sin. Rather than the biblical fact that I was in bondage to the sin of lust, I was labeled with a "disease" called "sexual addiction." I have a problem with this because I can repent of a sin, but I can't repent of a disease.

Also the counselor went on to claim that once a person is an addict, that person is always an addict. I have a problem with this also because he whom the Son sets free is free indeed (see John 8:36). Yet according to this counseling model, even if people do find a measure of freedom, they are considered to be in recovery for the rest of their lives.

I cannot imagine the apostle Paul sitting in a dank church basement talking about how he has been a recovering murderer for 20 years. Men, is this the level of freedom we are willing to accept simply because nobody has anything better to offer?

Tool 2: Motivating Factors

The tool that was used for motivation in the hands of the clinical approach was mainly fear: to be more specific, the fear of punishment. The counselor had each individual write up punishments that he would use on himself if he operated in lust. For example, "If I view pornography, I will give $100 to a political cause I don't believe in."

Over my years of study in the Word, I have found that there are only two ways to live—in love or in fear. *"There is no fear in love. But perfect love drives out fear, because fear has to do with punishment. The one who fears is not made perfect in love"* (1 John 4:18). Because we Christians know that we are called to walk in love, we cannot allow fear to be a part of our lives.

Punishment and fear are never healthy ways to motivate walking in true love; this would be like threatening children by saying that they must love you or else you will mercilessly beat them. The only way that children can learn to walk in love is through our displaying love to them as an example to follow. That is what God has done for us. *"We love Him because He first loved us"* (1 John 4:19 NKJV). And Romans 2:4 says that it is His kindness that brings us to repentance, not fear of punishment, guilt, or condemnation.

The idea that counselors could hang the fear of punishment over people's heads in the hopes of motivating them to walk in love was especially surprising and absurd. Jesus was the one who said, "If you love Me, you will obey Me" (see John 14:15). Therefore, love is the motivator for godly obedience, not fear.

Tool 3: Behavior Modification

The ability to force internal change through external pressure is a total myth. Imagine pushing a basketball underwater inside a swimming pool; the harder you push down, the more force the ball has in trying to surface. This is just as futile as the cycles of punishment that the clinical approach has adopted.

I was given a rubber band to put on my wrist and told to snap myself every time I had a lustful thought. I was told that I was totally powerless against my addiction/disease and that I would have to physically retrain my body and mind to walk in freedom. Christian counseling promised me that external regulations and behavioral modifications would be able to keep my sin nature in check. But this is not the *"free indeed"* (John 8:36) that Jesus promised. And I was not willing to settle for this nonsense.

I remember sitting next to "John" in a Sex Addicts Anonymous group when he shared that he had been in recovery for 14 years and that he had been sober (had not masturbated) for two years. The man on the other side of John congratulated him and asked him why he didn't seem happy about such an accomplishment. Then John broke down in tears and exclaimed, "I have been at these meetings multiple times a week for 14 years. I have been sober for two years, but I do not feel any freer! I still constantly have lustful thoughts and view women in evil ways. I want to be changed inside, but the behavioral modifications have only changed my outside reality, not my inside struggle. I don't want to go on like this."

"John" is like many Christian men. He has tried everything the Church has had to offer, but is in a state of despair that the methods and the freedom that have been offered him are far below the freedom that the Bible promises. Personally, I believe the Bible has the answers that men have been longing for in this area for many years. It is time to dig deep and lay the axe to the root of this bondage once and for all!

IDENTITY SHIFT

My approach to lasting freedom is based on changing the identity of the one in bondage to lust. As you read this book, you will find that your understanding of identity will be challenged. You will be stretched doctrinally and experientially. You will need to make major shifts in heart and mind.

Most people have formed their identity around their actions: "I do plumbing; therefore, I am a plumber." "I sin; therefore, I am a sinner." "I can't stop thinking lustful thoughts; therefore, I am a sex addict."

The truth is that your identity is not the sum total of your actions; identity is the foundation of your life from which your actions flow. For example, if you were born and raised in Spain, then your identity is that of a Spanish citizen who most likely speaks Spanish. Identity comes before actions, and actions flow forth from identity. Rightly stated: "I am righteous in Christ; therefore, I live righteously." *Identity always precedes actions.*

Identity is made of three components: the mind, the heart, and revelation. The mind represents all of the thinking that a person has processed. The heart contains all of the experiences that a person has had. Revelation is the place where the heart and mind have come into agreement to form a foundational belief system. *Identity flows out of a person's revelation.*

Imagine, for example, a young boy who is told every day that he is worthless. Certain thoughts form in the boy's mind. Also, if the boy is slapped and abused regularly, the experiences are stored within his heart. The combination of his heart and mind leads to a revelation that says, "You are worthless. You are trash. You don't matter. Your actions don't matter. There is no God. You should just do whatever you want because nobody will hold you accountable." And on the basis of this revelation, the identity of a criminal flows forth!

Biblically, we can observe how this identity transition took place in the life of Saul of Tarsus. On the road to Damascus, Saul had a revelation of Jesus that challenged his heart and mind—he had a tremendous experience that left him blind for three days (see Acts 9:1-30). I would imagine that in those three days he had his heart and mind come into agreement to form a new foundational belief system—one founded on the truth that Jesus is the Christ.

His new revelation caused him to have a new identity so that, after this shift, he was willing to die for Christ, whereas four days earlier he had been willing to kill those who believed in the Christ. It is amazing how quickly people's identities can change when their hearts and minds align and form a new revelation.

If identity flows out of revelation, then to change your identity, you must get a new revelation! To get a new revelation, you first have to renew your mind with truth and allow new experiences into your heart. This book and the tools within are designed to give you the truths and experiences you need to receive a new revelation and identity.

Tool

Which of the following paths have you tried? Based on a scale of effectiveness from one to ten (one indicating extreme ineffectiveness and ten signifying extreme effectiveness), how would you rate your experience?

• *Deliverance*	
• *Suppressing the soul*	
• *Battling the flesh nature*	
• *Internet filtering*	
• *Introspection*	
• *Inner healing*	
• *Managing your sexual appetite*	
• *12-step approach*	
• *Professional counseling*	

Ready for something better?

SECTION 1

WHO AM I?

The typical man struggling against impurity is actually caught in an identity crisis. Many feel like the man who said, *"...For what I want to do I do not do, but what I hate I do....What a wretched man I am! Who will rescue me from this body that is subject to death?"* (Rom. 7:15,24).

Men have been told that they are powerless against sin and will have to struggle with it for the rest of their lives. Some continue to try killing their old flesh nature, while others believe that their actions accumulate and form their identity. Essentially, Christian men don't know who they are, and this is why they don't live rightly. Once a man can get a revelation of himself as a new creation in Christ, then the right identity and lifestyle will be secured within him.

CHAPTER 2

YOU ARE POWERFUL

Only connect! That was the whole of her sermon.
Only connect the prose and the passion, and both
will be exalted, and human love will be seen
at its height. Live in fragments no longer.
—E.M. FORSTER, *Howards End*

I recently heard a well-known Christian motivational speaker who does marriage seminars around the country discuss the affects of sexual immorality on a person and a marriage. He suggested that, though change and healing are possible, the person who has had extramarital sexual experiences will always struggle with ungodly desires at some level. Such people will always need to be on guard and extra vigilant against temptation. And they will always have a degree of dysfunction in the ways that they view sex.

For many, this has been absolutely true. Yet his absolutism aroused some righteous anger in me. This is the exact mentality that informs most secular and Christian counseling on this subject. And, while (in the case of Christian resources) it is framed by the message of hope in Jesus, this belief system offers no actual hope.

Psalm 27:13 says: *"I would have despaired unless I had believed that I would see the goodness of the Lord in the land of the living"* (NASB). Many Christian men struggling with temptation and sexual sin feel despair for this exact reason. They do not believe they will see the goodness of God (total healing and freedom) in this area of their lives while they live on this Earth.

Not unlike this Christian speaker, the main premise of the 12-step programs is the *power of addiction.* In order to get help, one must admit to being a helpless and broken addict. It becomes a person's identity. "My name is Frank, and I am an addict." You no longer *have* a problem; you *are* the problem. You are a victim of a disease; you are a problem to be fixed.

Inspiring, isn't it? After years of struggling against temptations— trying not to check out that scantily dressed woman, look at that magazine in the grocery store checkout line, click on that pop-up advertisement for a porn site—most men reach a point of hopelessness. They feel powerless over sin, believing that they are controlled by outside forces and that no real answers are available. This belief is reinforced by resources on the subject. Thus, these men find themselves in the loneliest and most terrifying of places—despair. They feel like silent victims to their appetites, and they have relinquished all hope of rescue.

Sound familiar?

At the foundation of my approach to living free from sexual temptation is the belief that *you are powerful.* This approach is fundamentally opposite of the secular/clinical approach. As Step #1 of the 12-step recovery plan of Sex Addicts Anonymous states: "We admitted we were powerless over addictive sexual behavior—that our lives had become unmanageable."[1] This is the foundation of the clinical approach to dealing with sin: You are a sex *addict,* and the road to recovery begins when you admit that you are powerless over your *addiction.* Although this approach may help many men modify their behavior, it does not bring healing to the root issues in the heart.

During the time of the judges in the Old Testament, Israel experienced oppression from the Midianites (*Midian* means "strife"[2]). This was not simple border skirmishing, but absolute demoralization and terrorization of the people. For seven years, whenever Israel would plant crops, as harvest time approached, the Midianites would sweep through and destroy all of the crops, as well as the animals that the Israelites would use for both labor and food.

The Bible compares the Midianites to locusts that would come in swarms to devastate the land. Because of this, the people of Israel hid in caves and mountains and were brought very low (see Judg. 6:1-6). Let's put this scenario in modern terms: You are trying to live uprightly for God, yet it seems like whenever you begin to make progress or gain a measure of victory (plant seed) the enemy of temptation sweeps in to devastate your victory. You feel powerless to resist. You try to find a refuge, a hiding place, but you cannot escape the reality that once again your harvest has been stolen. Gradually, you lose all hope for the future.

Enter the hero—Gideon, a man much like you and me. Gideon was threshing wheat in a wine press in an attempt to hide his harvest from the Midianites. Gideon's name means "one who cuts to pieces"; he was supposed to be a warrior, a powerful man; yet he was defeated, hiding, and full of despair. Even though Gideon did not understand his identity, God did. The angel of the Lord appeared to Gideon, called him a powerful and brave man, and commissioned him to destroy the idol worship in Israel and defeat the Midianites through God's empowerment (see Judg. 6:6-16).

Though Gideon was full of excuses about why he was not the right man for the job (including self-pity, blame, and a victim mentality), God persistently spoke to him according to his destiny and identity in God—mighty man, brave warrior, conqueror of strife. Ultimately, Gideon chose to believe God's assessment of him and stepped into his destiny, winning a great victory. (There is much I am leaving out here, but the entire story, which is found in Judges 6, is very powerful and worth reading.)

Many Bible scholars believe the angel of the Lord who appears in various places in the Old Testament is actually Jesus—God manifested to humanity before Jesus' incarnation. Thus, we can read Gideon's story into our lives this way. When we feel oppressed by sin and temptation, Jesus speaks to us about our true destiny and identity in Him, and He calls us to take responsibility and act powerfully according to that identity.

When Gideon believed what God said about him and acted accordingly, he found freedom. And you can too. In this book you will find the truth about who you are. You are not an addict—a helpless and hopeless victim of addiction. No, you are a son of God. And you are powerful. In the coming pages I will show you what that means and how a revelation of your identity can absolutely free you from the struggle with sexual sin.

JESUS RESTORES OUR POWER AND VALUE

Though the clinical approach says that complete freedom is a myth, Jesus died to give humanity absolute freedom from and power over sin. He did not intend for us to struggle against lust all of our lives. Instead, He said, *"If the Son makes you free, you will be free indeed"* (John 8:36 NASB).

Jesus illustrated this in His response to the woman caught in adultery (see John 8:1-11). Though the woman had been caught *"in the very act"* (John 8:4 NASB) and could have been condemned to death according to the law, Jesus instead spoke to her according to her value. He said, *"I do not condemn you..."* (John 8:11 NASB)—in other words,

He didn't label her as adulterous, but instead valued her as a loved daughter of God. And He called her to be powerful, to take responsibility and make a choice—*"...Go. From now on sin no more"* (John 8:11 NASB).

This is exactly what Jesus has done for us. Through His death on the cross He has said, *"I do not condemn you"* (I value you); and through His resurrection, *"Go. From now on sin no more"* (you are powerful and able to live holy). We have been given the power to walk in purity and freedom. We do not, as so many Christians believe, have to wrestle with sin all of our lives.

Referring to his freedom, the apostle Paul said that he would not allow anything to control him—*"...I will not be mastered by anything"* (1 Cor. 6:12). This was not just wishful thinking. He could say this because through grace we have literally been given the power to reign in life and to operate in self-control (see Rom. 5:17; Titus 2:11-14). The death and resurrection of Christ are more than sufficient for every need, every weakness, and every sin in our lives.

As I alluded to in the stories of Gideon and the woman caught in adultery, there are two foundational principles that we must understand in order to walk in freedom and self-control: *I am powerful,* and *I am valuable.* We will explore both of these principles, starting with the first: you are powerful.

POWERFUL PEOPLE ARE SELF-CONTROLLED

Jesus said that everyone who sins is a slave to sin (see John 8:34); but then He died so we would no longer be controlled by sin, but would instead have self-control. Remember that John the Baptist described Jesus as *"the Lamb of God, who takes away the sin of the world"* (John 1:29).

Remember also that Paul commanded believers, saying:

Therefore do not let sin reign in your mortal body so that you obey its lusts....For sin shall not be master over you, for you are not under law but under grace (Romans 6:12,14 NASB).

As those who have accepted Christ's sacrifice for our sins, we are under grace, and we, therefore, have a choice. We are powerful. Paul said, *"Do not let...,"* implying that the believer now has the power to choose against sin. We are not victims or slaves of sin as we once were. If we sin, it is because we choose to.

Another example of the choice we must make is seen in the story of Cain and Abel. *"The Lord said to Cain '...sin is crouching at your door; it desires to have you, but you must rule over it'"* (Gen. 4:6-7). Notice that God did not say that sin was within Cain and that he had no choice but to obey its whims. Choice is always a factor.

However, Paul also said in Romans 6 that when we do choose to sin, we give sin the throne in our lives (sin reigns and we obey). So although we are powerful and free because of Christ, we allow sin to be our master. When we choose lust, we are giving up self-control and selling our freedom to the old flame, the porn star, the stripper, or the prostitute. We must value our freedom enough to choose self-control.

When we choose self-control, God's grace empowers us to maintain that choice. Jesus Christ provided grace through His death and resurrection. Though people often group *mercy* and *grace* together, their concepts are not synonymous. Many of us have heard the difference defined like this: *Mercy* is not getting what we deserve (death), and *grace* is getting what we don't deserve (life). Grace literally empowers believers to walk in all that God has designed them to walk in. God's grace is a gift to us that enables us to live victorious lives here and now. Once we begin to receive God's grace as a gift that empowers us, we will reign in life. Romans 5:17 says that Jesus provides us with an abundant provision of empowering grace so that we may reign—so that we may fulfill our call of living like Christ:

For if, by the trespass of the one man, death reigned through that one man, how much more will those who receive God's abundant provision of grace and of the gift of righteousness reign in life through the one man, Jesus Christ! (Romans 5:17)

It is important to note that Jesus provided us with righteousness, not as something achieved by works, but as a gift received by faith. Though many of us understand this concept with our minds, we still live as though we were trying to be righteous on our own. We try really hard, but inevitably we fail because we are acting apart from God's grace.

So what does it mean to receive righteousness by faith (and not by trying hard)? We must realize that when God looks at us, He now sees the righteousness of Christ. Romans 4:5 says: *"But to the one who does not work, but believes in Him who justifies the ungodly, his faith is credited as righteousness"* (NASB). In His eyes, we are blameless and holy. That is our current identity because of Christ.

When we choose to believe what God says about us, we are enabled to receive His grace for righteous living. When we accept His truth about us, we no longer strive for approval through works; neither do we condemn ourselves by evaluating our potential based on our history. Rather, we simply accept God's declaration of our righteousness. As God renews our minds according to this truth, we will begin to access the grace to live righteously.

GRACE EMPOWERS SELF-CONTROL

Not only has God given us grace, but He has also given us the gift of His Holy Spirit living within us, who brings the fruit of self-control (see Gal. 5:22-23). This means that we have personal responsibility and freedom. It is absolutely incredible to realize that God wants us to be free. He doesn't want to control us, as He has proven since the beginning, when He put two trees in the Garden of Eden. Pastor Danny Silk explains it well:

> In the beginning, God created mankind to be free. There were no constraints in the Garden. Adam and Eve were running around naked (see Gen. 2:25)—no bras, no underwear, no bathing suits, nothing. This is God's intended version of your life: absolute freedom. But what made the Garden free? It wasn't that they were naked. No, the Garden was free because of the Tree of the Knowledge of Good and Evil. "What?" you ask. "That's the bad tree! How could that lead them to freedom?" Well, if they hadn't had the Tree of the Knowledge of Good and Evil in that Garden, they would have been trapped in a paradise prison. Without the option of making a poor choice in that environment, they would not have been free.[3]

As we know, Adam and Eve made the wrong choice and traded their freedom for sin. But God valued our freedom so much that He sent Jesus to purchase it back for us through His death on the cross.

Yes, our freedom is worth the death of Jesus because God intends that we use all that He has given us so that we will reign in life. Like Romans 5:17 says, we *"who receive God's abundant provision of grace and of the gift of righteousness reign in life through the one man, Jesus Christ!"* Now that Jesus has accomplished His work on our behalf, we have been given grace, which teaches us how to walk in self-control. Because of Jesus' grace and freedom, we never have to be controlled by outside forces. Rather, grace empowers us to operate in self-control:

> *For the **grace of God** has appeared that offers salvation to all people. It **teaches us to say "No" to ungodliness** and **worldly passions**, and **to live self-controlled, upright and godly lives** in this present age, while we wait for the blessed*

*hope—the appearing of the glory of our great God and Savior, Jesus Christ, who gave Himself for us to redeem us from all wickedness and **to purify for Himself a people that are his very own, eager to do what is good*** (Titus 2:11-14).

If we do not understand that our self-control is empowered by the grace of God, then we will try to control our flesh by the strength of our flesh, and this will always fail. Jesus has provided the fruit of the Spirit for us; without the Spirit, we can't operate in His fruit. For those trying to enact their own righteousness through works, this list can feel like the most awful of standards. Only God's grace enables us to walk in any of the fruit, including self-control.

THE POWER OF CHOICE

To the man struggling with lust, the most irritating of the nine fruit of the Spirit is self-control. He may feel that he is doing well in the other eight, but self-control eludes him.

Many have described *self-control* as "the ability to say no to sin." Under this definition, the man struggling with lust will feel like a daily failure. Yet this definition of self-control is inherently flawed because of its narrowness. Self-control is not simply the ability to say no to sin. I would propose that the definition of *self-control* is better expressed as "my being the only one who determines my responses in life." This shift of definition has far-reaching implications. In the past when we were controlled by fear or lust, there were forces of sin that literally ran our lives and controlled us. Not only has their control been removed by Jesus' death on the cross, but we also have been given back the reins of our own lives. That is what *self-control* means.

You are powerful because God has given you self-control. Self-control gives you the power of choice. If you are controlled by outside forces, then your decisions are not truly your own; therefore, you are not operating in freedom. Once you begin to walk in self-control, you realize that you are *the only one* controlling your life and decisions; therefore, you become able to make powerful choices. Powerful people are not controlled by outside forces. They literally command and direct their own decisions, and they take full responsibility for their own actions and consequences.

Jesus' intention was for His followers to have the freedom to walk in self-control and to be powerful people. About this, Paul wrote:

> *It was for freedom that Christ set us free; therefore keep standing firm and do not be subject again to a yoke of slavery....For you were called to freedom, brethren; only do not turn your freedom into an opportunity for the flesh, but through love serve one another* (Galatians 5:1,13 NASB).

Here Paul clearly connects freedom with self-control and the ability to choose powerfully. He exhorts us to choose love rather than returning to slavery to sin. This call to powerful decision-making comes just before Paul's list of the fruit of the Spirit. Jesus has called us to freedom, and we live out that freedom by making powerful decisions based on the truth of God's Word and the characteristics (fruit) of the Spirit. We are no longer subject to the yoke of our whims or emotions or desires; rather, we are actually able to choose love, no matter the circumstance.

When we are mistreated, self-control does not simply keep us from responding wrongly, but it also gives us the power to respond rightly, in love. The old definition of *self-control* only gave us the power to say no to wrongdoing. The new definition empowers us to say no to wrongdoing *and* make the choice to walk proactively in love.

For a man tempted to embrace sexual sin, this is not just "bouncing" his eyes or beating his flesh into submission, but truly considering the needs of the people in his life (his wife, his children, his parents, the women he is tempted to objectify, and so forth) and being compelled by his and Christ's love for them. Self-control manifested in love looks like this: A man who's tempted to go to a strip club, instead asks the Lord for His heart for the girls who work there. Receiving the revelation that they are loved, but deeply-wounded daughters of God, he begins praying for their salvation and healing. Perhaps he even sends them flowers from God.

Here's another scenario: A married man sits in front of his computer feeling tempted to look at pornography; instead, he asks God to show him how He sees his wife. From that revelation of love, he not only chooses against clicking on the wrong sites, but also decides to surprise his wife with a meaningful expression of his value for her. We will discuss this more in the third section entitled, "Who Is She?"

The truth of self-control is that you are powerful and you can always choose to control yourself. Self-control means that nothing outside of you is running your life—not your angry boss, your rebellious children, your nagging wife, your critical mother-in-law, the evil spirits of lust, generational curses, the wounds from your past, or anything else. Absolutely nothing can control you because the Holy Spirit gave the reins of your life back to you. This is an awesome and empowering truth!

You are in charge of you. First Corinthians 9:25 says, *"Everyone who competes in the games exercises self-control in all things. They then do it to receive a perishable wreath, but we an imperishable"* (NASB). Paul highlights self-control as the key to victory, and through Jesus' blood, you now possess that key. Victory over sexual temptation is possible because you have been given self-control—because you are a powerful person.

Nobody can make you angry. You have the power to choose how to respond when others injure you. Nobody can steal your peace. You always get to choose how to respond. You are the only one in control of you. Nobody can make you follow your lustful thoughts. You always get to make the choice. The lie that counselors teach is that you are out of control. You are not out of control; you are just making stupid choices with the control that you have been given. You are choosing to return to that *"yoke of slavery"* (Gal. 5:1). But you don't have to.

You get to choose how to live your life. You can respond with kindness and forgiveness, or anger and bitterness. It is always your choice, and nobody can force you to choose differently. Paul and Silas chose to sing hymns and pray after being unjustly beaten and imprisoned (see Acts 16:22-25). When David's city was raided, all of the women and children were taken captive, and his men talked of stoning him in their despair; David instead chose to strengthen himself in God's goodness (see 1 Sam. 30:1-6). When Corrie Ten Boom, a Holocaust survivor, encountered one of the soldiers who had years earlier killed her sister, she chose to forgive him and welcome that repentant soldier into the family of God.[4] These people and many others have made powerful choices, whether in the midst of incredible adversity or in the face of daily stresses and temptations. You can too.

When you see an attractive woman, nobody can make you lust; it is merely a choice. You could choose not to lust, but unless you realize that you are in charge of yourself, you will live as a victim. When you live without self-control, you will constantly be fighting with overwhelming outside forces. Paul the apostle wrote:

> *"I have the right to do anything," you say—but not everything is beneficial. "I have the right to do anything"—but **I will not be mastered by anything"** (1 Corinthians 6:12).

Paul was a powerful person who understood that *self-control meant that nothing outside of him could control him.* Only you are controlling you; no one else is responsible for the decisions you make. The Holy Spirit has given you self-control, and like Paul, you can choose to *"not be mastered by anything."*

YOU ARE BETTER THAN THAT!

This reminds me of a scene from the boxing movie, *Rocky Balboa*. Rocky had recently decided to come out of retirement to fight the leading and undefeated world champion. The media is predicting Rocky's humiliating loss. Rocky's adult son, Robert, has lived his whole life in his father's shadow and is struggling to make it in the corporate world. In fear of his own reputation being tarnished, Robert comes by Rocky's restaurant to ask his father not to go back into boxing. You can see from their conversation that Robert doesn't feel like he is in control of his own life. (Be sure to read the following dialogue in true Rocky fashion, with a Philly accent).

Robert: So you are going through with this?

Rocky: Yeah, I start training tomorrow.

Robert: So are you nervous about the fight?

Rocky: I am scared to death.

Robert: You don't look scared.

Rocky: Well, you're not supposed to.

Robert: You don't have to do it.

Rocky: Yeah, well, I think I do.

Robert: You know, livin' with you, it hasn't been easy. People see me, but they think of you! Now with all this going on, it is going to be worse than ever!

Rocky: It don't have to be.

Robert: Yeah, sure it does!

Rocky: Why? You have got a lot going on for you, kid!

Robert: What, my last name? That's the reason I got a good job, that's the reason that people deal with me in the first place. Now, I start to get ahead, I start to get a little something for myself, and this happens! Now, I am asking you, as a favor, not to go through with this. This is only going to end up bad for you, and it is only going to end up bad for me.

Rocky: You think I am hurting you?

Robert: Yeah, in a way you are!

Rocky: That is the last thing that I ever wanted to do.

Robert: I know that is not what you wanted to do, but that is just the way that it is! Don't you care what people think? Doesn't it bother you that people are making you out to be a joke and that I am going to be included in that? Do you think that's right? Do you?

(Rocky pauses.)

Rocky: You ain't gonna believe this, but you used to fit right here (pointing to the palm of his hand). I used to hold you up and say to your mother, this kid's going to be the best kid in the world.

(Robert rolls his eyes.)

Rocky: This kid is going to be somebody better than anybody I ever knew. And you grew up good and wonderful. It was great just watching you and every day was like a privilege. Then, the time came for you to be your own man and take on the world. And you did...but somewhere along the way you changed, you stopped being you. You let people stick a finger in your face and tell you that you're no good! And when things got hard you started looking for something to blame, like a big shadow. Let me tell you something you already know; the world ain't all sunshine and rainbows. It is a very mean and nasty place and I don't care how tough you are, it will beat you to your knees and keep you there permanently if you let it. You, me, or nobody else is gonna hit us as hard as life. But it ain't about how hard you can hit, it's about how hard you can get hit and keep moving forward, how much you can take and keep moving forward! That's how winnin' is done! Now, if you know what you are worth, go out and get what you are worth! But you have gotta be willing to take the hits! And not be pointing fingers saying that you are not where you wanna be because of him, or her, or anybody! Cowards do that. And that ain't you! You are better than that! I am always going to love you no matter what, no matter what happens. You are my son, you are my blood, you are the best thing in my life. But until you begin believing in yourself, you ain't gonna have a life.[5]

Rocky was not only physically strong, he was also emotionally strong. He had a high level of self-control. Even while his son was yelling at him, he spoke words of unconditional love, honor, and strength into Robert. Rocky is a beautiful picture of the power of self-control. He made choices based on his own heart and was not swayed by the fear of what others would say or do. His son, Robert, however, had become a coward by living as if he was not in control of his own life. Robert lived as a victim of outside forces.

THE VICTIM MINDSET

People who do not understand this concept of self-control feel powerless and, like Rocky's son Robert, believe themselves to be victims of their circumstances. While some people do become victims of circumstance in an outward sense, the reality is that they still have a choice about their inward response to those circumstances. It may be difficult to hear, but even those who suffer from the most horrendous crimes—such as rape, the murder of a loved one, torture, and so forth—must face the reality of their personal responsibility to choose their response and their ability to choose either hatred, anger, and bitterness, or love, mercy, and forgiveness. This is certainly not an easy choice, and I in no way intend to undermine the pain of victimization. Yet the fact remains that we all have a choice, no matter our circumstance or struggle.

Viktor Frankl, an Austrian Jewish author and psychiatrist, suffered in the Auschwitz concentration camp of Nazi Germany. During that time, as everything he valued and based his identity upon was stripped from him, he came to a powerful realization, which he writes about in his book *Man's Search for Meaning*. The following excerpt is quoted in an article by Uri Paz:

> A person is not an object among other objects. Objects determine each other's path. A human being, on the other hand, is graced with the power of self-definition. His path and his destiny—of course within the framework of his abilities and environment—he decides himself. In the concentration camps, in that living laboratory, we saw some of our comrades behaving like pigs and others behaving like saints. Both alternatives are hidden in a person; and which will be realized depends on decisions and not on conditions.[6]

Though Frankl was outwardly a victim of Nazi brutality, inwardly he realized his ability to be powerful and chose to walk in forgiveness toward his captors.

Regardless of circumstances, people who feel powerless and who do not operate in self-control will refuse to take personal responsibility for their lives. They will continually play the blame game. They will blame a sin nature, the devil, those tempting women, their parents, and so forth. Only when you understand that only you are in control of yourself, can you fix your problem. You were powerful enough to choose sin; therefore, you are powerful enough to choose not to sin. You are not a victim; you are not powerless. No, you are powerful. You are powerful because you are the only one who controls you. Nothing and nobody outside of your skin can cause you to sin. Self-control means that you are responsible for your own choices, feelings, actions, and reactions. Either you have self-control or, like Robert Balboa, you are playing the victim and allowing everyone else to run your life.

TAKING RESPONSIBILITY FOR FREEDOM

Self-control is essential to personal freedom. If you want to live in freedom, you must take responsibility for your life by choosing to be self-controlled and powerful. Imagine a red-faced man who is angry and yelling. Imagine him getting up in your face, poking you with his finger, and cursing you out. Imagine he's attacking your character, accusing you of being dishonest or greedy or stupid. How would you respond? Would you get angry and yell back? Would you emotionally withdraw and walk away feeling hurt and bitter? Would you try to appease him with excuses and blame-shifting? Or would you act like a powerful, self-controlled man who knows he's his own boss and is responsible for his own decisions? When you have self-control, you can calmly listen to the angry man, hear his heart, and thoughtfully respond. Without self-control, you become manipulated by and afraid of his anger, and you live a reactive life. God gave you self-control so that you would always be free to respond under your own power, rather than living reactively.

POWERFUL PEOPLE ARE ASSERTIVE

Being a self-controlled person who takes responsibility for his life is the first step to freedom. The second step is to understand how powerful people deal with their inward lives in order to remain emotionally and relationally healthy.

People who are not self-controlled usually have dysfunctional relationships and fear true intimacy. Because they do not believe that they are the only ones who have control of their lives, they fear that transparency will enable others to control them. Thus, they create façades and play control games. As powerless people, because of hurt or fear, they compulsively hide. However, Second Timothy 1:7 says, *"For God didn't give us a spirit of fear, but of power, love, and self-control"* (WEB). Powerful people choose to open their hearts and share their feelings.

As terrifying as it might seem, the most powerful thing you can do is be open, honest, and vulnerable. The apostle Paul, as a powerful person, modeled this to the Corinthian church and exhorted them to also open their hearts to him:

> *We have spoken freely to you, Corinthians, **and opened wide our hearts to you**. We are not withholding our affection from you, but you are withholding yours from us. As a fair exchange—I speak as to my children—**open wide your hearts also*** (2 Corinthians 6:11-13).

MADE FOR INTIMACY

As humans, we are made for intimate and transparent relationships. I'm not speaking of sexual intimacy, though that is part of intimacy within marriage; rather I'm speaking of the intimate and transparent sharing of thoughts and emotions—letting another person "see into" us. Not only did God make us to be intimate with Himself, but also to have transparent relationships with each other.

We are at our best when we have a safe environment in which we can be vulnerable. However, most people have had hurtful experiences that suggest an emotional link between transparency and the fear of rejection or pain. Because of this, they become self-protected and emotionally disconnected. Though they long to be transparent and to experience intimacy because it is part of their design, they hide from it because of fear.

Many attempt to fill their relationship-void with things rather than people; this counterfeit intimacy is called *addiction*—an emotional bond with an object or substance (which they can control) rather than a person (whom they cannot control). The irony, of course, is that ultimately such people give the control of their lives to the object of their addiction.

As part of the decision to be powerful people, we must embrace intimacy, which is a crucial aspect of the freedom of self-control that Jesus purchased for us. Healthy intimacy and freedom cannot be separated. Among powerless people, the goal of communication is to convince others, to control them by forcing agreement. As powerful people, we understand that we cannot control others, but only ourselves.

The flip side of this is the liberating realization that others cannot control us, which means that we do not need to fear being emotionally intimate with them. We are free to share our hearts because we know that we will not be controlled by their responses. Thus, the goal in communication becomes understanding and connecting. Because we are self-controlled, we are able to seek to understand what is going on inside of another person without feeling the need to control that person in order to protect our own emotions.

> *There is no fear in love. But perfect love drives out fear, because fear has to do with punishment. The one who fears is not made perfect in love* (1 John 4:18).

The intimacy and safety of perfect love (of which self-control is a part) casts out fear. The converse is also true. Fear casts out love and disables intimacy. As powerful people, we choose not to fear other people and their responses. We know they can't control us, and we know we can't control them. Rather, we choose to act in love by opening our hearts and seeking to establish healthy connection.

COMMUNICATION TYPES

The differences between healthy, powerful communication and unhealthy, powerless communication are outlined in the four standard communication types: Aggressive, Passive, Passive-Aggressive, and Assertive. The first three are dysfunctional and powerless; only the fourth, Assertive, provides an emotionally healthy option. Here is a simple way to define these based on the unspoken motto of each type:

- Passive—"You matter. I don't."

- Aggressive—"I matter. You don't."

- Passive-Aggressive—"You matter...*not!*"

- Assertive—"You matter. So do I."

Passive and Aggressive are complementary communication types. Passive people are afraid of rejection, of the accusation of selfishness, and of conflict. Therefore, passive people simply give way to the people around them; often they do this in the name of "laying down their lives for others" just like Jesus did. Let me be clear: Jesus did not passively allow others to walk all over Him. The Bible says that no one could take His life from Him, but that He chose to lay it down because it was His Father's will (see John 10:17-18). At no other time during His earthly life did Jesus "lay down" before the demands of others. Rather, He consistently made powerful choices based on the Father's will and not on popular opinion.

Passive communication in the name of Jesus is simply the spiritualization of fear. The reality is that people who communicate passively are unable to experience intimacy because they allow no one to know what they really believe or feel. Unfortunately, over time this communication style often creates people who feel used, neglected, disrespected, powerless, and resentful. Passive people are the quintessential victims, believing themselves subject to the whims of others. In order to find freedom, they need to acknowledge their power to choose, and they need to take responsibility for the dysfunction they contribute to relationships through their refusal to open their hearts in intimacy.

The Aggressive communication style pairs well with the Passive because aggressive people are very efficient at invalidating the needs of the people around them. They don't trust anyone and never open their hearts to others. Rather, their bottom line is getting what they want, often through control and forcefulness.

Passive-Aggressive, as the name implies, is a combination of the first two. Passive-aggressive people pretend to care about others. Their communication resembles the Passive style, but they make sure they get their way through subtle manipulation, including sarcasm, innuendo, double meanings, and unclear communication. Sadly, this communication style is often the most acceptable attitude within the Church.

Each of these three communication types promotes anxiety, guardedness, and selfishness. Relationships founded on one or more of these styles will lack trust, connection, safety, and nurturing because the people involved are not self-controlled, but are reacting in various ways to the fear of transparency.

In contrast to these is the Assertive communication style. Assertive people value understanding and mutual respect; thus, they hold themselves responsible to maintain respect levels and to protect healthy communication. They value both their own feelings and the feelings of others, thereby creating a dynamic in which there are no victims and no opponents, but rather fully-valued humans in conversation. This type of communication creates a safe place for vulnerable sharing of emotions, including being gut-level honest about hurts and fears.

Such people make the powerful choice to listen to others, to sincerely care about how they feel, and to endeavor to understand. They also choose to act powerfully by courageously sharing from their hearts. Thus they are sources of strength and comfort, leading to true biblical intimacy. Clearly, as people who are self-controlled and powerful, we have only one acceptable communication style—Assertive.[7]

IN SYMPHONY

When we open our hearts, we form connections with other people. As we do that, we must learn to understand and protect those connections.[8] Although for many people, the primary goal in relationships is to protect themselves from being hurt; as powerful people, one of our primary goals must be protecting the connections we form with others. Those connections in Scripture are called harmony, which is translated from the Greek word *sumphonea*, which literally means "to sound together."[9] It is often also translated as "agreement" or "concord."

From *sumphonea,* we get our English word *symphony.* Most of us have heard at the very least a portion of a recorded musical symphony, yet we might not realize that one of the distinguishing characteristics of symphonies is their length and the complexity and variety of sound. When applied to other areas of life, *symphony* can be simply defined as something with "harmonious complexity and variety."[10]

Applying this word to our connections, we can see that powerful relationships are characterized by an appreciation of complexity (depth) and variety (differences). In harmonious relationships we do not try to force agreement or assimilation, but are able to savor our uniqueness and the ways our various "sounds" (personalities, opinions, passions, and so forth) flow together to make something beautiful. Of course, the beauty comes only as we express our individuality within the harmonious structure. In other words, we have to maintain respect and love through self-control and powerful communication.

> *Bless those who persecute you; bless and do not curse. Rejoice with those who rejoice; mourn with those who mourn.* **Live in harmony with one another.** *Do not be proud, but be willing*

to associate with people of low position. Do not be conceited (Romans 12:14-16).

In Romans, Paul commands us to live in harmony with one another, yet, as we have seen, this is not simply the absence of fighting. *Harmony* indicates strength of relationship, an intertwining. Harmony is a symphony of people in healthy, powerful relationships. Such harmony—which really is like the masterful coordination of sounds and instruments that creates a beautiful composition—must be nurtured, cultivated, and protected in order to be sustained.

Many people live in complete disharmony with their friends and spouses because of fear. They feel controlled by outside forces, and fear keeps them from opening their hearts and powerfully communicating their feelings and needs. They fear how others will respond so they close their hearts. We do not have to live this way. No matter how many times we have been hurt, we still have choices. We all have the opportunity to walk in harmony in our relationships and to be connected heart-to-heart, but we must choose to walk through the fear of being open and assertive. That is the powerful choice that will lead to health and harmony.

JACOB'S CHOICE

Let's examine a practical example of how the communication types play out. The patriarch Jacob and his birth family aptly illustrate the first three communication types (see Gen. 25–30), and the unexpected end of their story demonstrates the redemptive power of Assertive communication.

Their story's dysfunctions and powerless power struggles are similar to many of ours. Isaac, Jacob's father, takes the Passive role. Though he is the head of the family, he fails to reprimand Esau for being aggressive or Jacob and Rebekah for being manipulative. Instead, he seems to be pulled along by the current of events created by the other members of his family. The counterpart of Isaac's Passive style is Esau, the Aggressive eldest son (see Gen. 27:41). Not surprisingly, he is the favored son who has his father "wrapped around his little finger."

Struggling against the Aggressive domination of Esau, we find Jacob, the younger brother, and Rebekah, their mother. In classic Passive-Aggressive style, Jacob and Rebecca enact a series of manipulative tactics to usurp Esau's place of control. First Jacob manipulates Esau into giving him his birthright (see Gen. 25:29-34). Later, Rebekah directs Jacob to manipulate Isaac by disguising himself as Esau (see Gen. 27:5-17). Jacob then deceives the blind and dying Isaac into believing that Jacob is actually Esau, and as a result, Jacob steals Esau's blessing from his father (see Gen. 27:18-38). Finally, Jacob manipulates his uncle Laban (who also demonstrates Passive-Aggressive tendencies) in order to claim the strongest and healthiest of Laban's flocks for himself (see Gen. 30:25-43). Jacob's relationships were a big, powerless mess.

But along the way, Jacob encounters God, gaining a revelation of himself that changes everything. After deceiving Laban, Jacob and his household travel back to their home in Canaan. On their way, they have to pass through the land where Esau now lives, and Jacob fears that his brother will take revenge on him. The night before he must meet Esau, Jacob pleads with God to deliver him. He also sends ahead presents for Esau in hopes of appeasing him (which is another manifestation of Passive-Aggressive behavior). In the night, however, the angel of the Lord comes to wrestle with Jacob, and through that encounter Jacob receives a new name—Israel—and a blessing from God (see Gen. 32). Though not many details are given, I think it is safe to assume that wrestling with God all night would have changed Jacob's perspective on many things. Certainly, he would have come to the conclusion that, if he could hold his ground in a divine wrestling match (as he did), he could begin to live a powerful, responsible life.

The next morning, the dreaded encounter with Esau occurs. Yet instead of the anger or blaming or manipulation we might expect, the two brothers communicate with sincerity and openness, even embracing and weeping in each other's arms. There is no mention of the past offenses, but only warmth and generosity. Rather than running or manipulating, they face each other directly, which is an unmistakable display of Assertive communication (see Gen. 33:1-16).

As evidenced in the life of Jacob, Assertive communication is the only healthy, powerful option. It requires opening the heart and risking vulnerability, knowing that even if others hurt you, they cannot control you. It cares about the needs of others rather than trying to control them. Bottom line: Powerful and assertive people value intimacy, and they are willing to risk getting hurt in order to create healthy connections. The three dysfunctional types of communication are self-protective, but they create separation. Because Assertive communication opens the heart and shares vulnerably about hurts and fears, it leads to great connections.

Many have become paralyzed in anger, hurt, or fear. These conditions keep them from opening their hearts and being assertive. Have we done the same? What has hurt us or scared us? What has kept us from communicating assertively with those we love? As powerful and self-controlled men, we must learn to walk in Assertive communication in order to manage our inner lives and maintain healthy relationships.

Tool 1

Write at least five answers to the following questions on a separate sheet of paper.

1. I feel powerless when... (for example, my boss is upset at me, etc.).

2. I feel controlled when... (for example, my wife speaks to me aggressively, etc.).

3. I blame others when... (for example, I am scared, etc.).

Tool 2

Now take the scenarios that you wrote about in Tool 1 and write out a powerful decision for each scenario such as:

1. I will choose to be powerful... (for example, by taking responsibility for my actions toward my boss).

2. I will choose self-control... (for example, by speaking assertively in love to my wife when she is being aggressive).

3. Rather than blaming, I choose to (for example, take responsibility, apologize, or be assertive, etc.).

Tool 3

Look at the four communication types and identify the following: In the past I have been: (circle one)

Aggressive   Passive   Passive/Aggressive   Assertive

Take the time to explain these four types to your spouse or a close friend (if you are single). Ask them which of the four they have seen in you. Ask them to give you examples.

List at least five character defects of the communication type that you have walked in. Next to them, list the five positive traits of Assertiveness that counteract the defects named.

Write out your action plan for each trait. Example: *When I feel like closing my heart and hiding in passivity, I will choose instead to be assertive and keep my heart open. I will make a powerful choice.*

CHAPTER 3

You Are Valuable

Give me liberty or give me death!
—Patrick Henry

I remember the first time I saw *Saving Private Ryan* in the theater. I also remember the fourth time I saw it in that setting. Each time, I sat with the audience stunned for at least ten minutes after the movie was over. *Saving Private Ryan* is best known for allowing the viewer to experience the sights and sounds of war right along with the soldiers storming the beach. Its realism caused the audience to catch a glimpse of the truth of the phrase, "war is hell."

> While *Saving Private Ryan* shows very vividly the horrors of war, this is not the main idea of the movie. The fictional story primarily revolves around Captain Miller (Tom Hanks) and his squad who are sent behind enemy lines to find Private James Ryan (Matt Damon), whose three brothers have been killed in combat. The main question raised is why eight men are risking their lives to save just one? As the movie progresses, we see this debate on several occasions.

First, we see General George Marshall, Army Chief of Staff, order a rescue squad be sent in to find Ryan and "get him the hell out of there." One member of his staff objects and claims that any members of a rescue squad would be killed trying to retrieve Ryan.

Second, we see the rescue squad itself debate the issue when the squad first embarks on its mission. Private Reiben (Edward Burns) inquires, "You wanna explain the math of this to me? I mean, where's the sense of riskin' the lives of the eight of us to save one guy?" In response, Captain Miller replies that soldiers must follow orders even if one believes the mission is "fubar." He goes on to tell Reiben, tongue in cheek, that the mission has a valuable objective and that he feels heartfelt sorrow for the mother of Private Ryan. At this point, we begin to see Captain Miller struggle with the issue of obeying orders when he's not convinced of the wisdom of those orders, and we are uncertain about his true beliefs regarding the worthiness of the mission.

Third, we see the squad encounter Captain Hamill (Ted Danson). Hamill states to Captain Miller that he understands their mission and tells them to find Ryan and get him home. The following scene shows Captain Miller debating the mission with his second in command, Sgt. Mike Horvath (Tom Sizemore). Miller says that Ryan had better be worth their efforts to find him; Ryan better cure some disease or invent the longer lasting light bulb because he would choose just one of the soldiers he has already lost over ten Ryans. Thus, we see Miller struggling even more with the wisdom of his orders.

Next we see Reiben's frustration with the mission finally spilling out after Wade is killed. He mocks Captain Miller's decision to attack a German outpost and says that he hopes Mama Ryan is proud that her son's life is worth more than the lives of two other soldiers. In order to diffuse the situation, Captain Miller says he doesn't care anything about Private Ryan. But if saving Private Ryan earns him the right to return home then he will carry out his mission. Thus, we now see Captain Miller seeking some sort of justification for his mission.

Finally, the squad finds Private Ryan and breaks the news to him of the deaths of his brothers. In a surprising twist, Ryan refuses to leave. He refuses to follow Miller's orders and instead chooses to follow the orders given, which was to hold the bridge at all costs. Miller decides to stay and help the soldiers hold the bridge and then get Ryan back to safety. After the final battle is over only two members of the original eight sent out to rescue Ryan survive. Just before he dies, Miller says to Ryan, "earn this." In other words, make the mission worth the sacrifice.[1]

Throughout the movie *Saving Private Ryan,* we see the struggle to understand the value of a man's life. As believers we know the answer to this question. Most of us haven't had eight soldiers die for us, but this does not even begin to compare to the fact that we have had the Son of God lay down His life for us. How valuable and priceless are we, according to the economics of Heaven, that the Father would lay down Jesus to redeem us?

Many Christians have lived with a self-deprecating faith that reinforces the idea that they have *no* value. This mindset is the devil's playground because people who don't understand their value will *not value others*. This value deficit is at the core of the lust problem. We don't value others because we don't value ourselves. Whether the perpetrator is a murderer, a rapist, or a watcher of pornography, the victim is devalued because the perpetrator doesn't understand that he is loved and valued by God. When we grasp how valuable and lovable we are, then we will love and value others.

HOW MUCH IS YOUR FREEDOM WORTH?

If we do not value ourselves and our personal freedom, we will sell our self-control to the highest bidder and become slaves to sin again. That was the problem with Esau. The writer of Hebrews compares sexually immoral people to Esau, who in a moment of hunger sold his birthright to his younger brother in exchange for some food: *"See that no one is sexually immoral, or is godless like Esau, who for a single meal sold his inheritance rights as the oldest son"* (Heb. 12:16).

As this passage indicates, the sexually immoral and Esau are alike in that both are willing to sell out for a moment of pleasure. They can be bought and sold for a price. They do not maintain self-control because they do not value their freedom. Instead, they have given into the power of lust and the cravings of their bodies.

To illustrate my point, imagine the following scenario. The most beautiful woman that you have ever seen comes to you and states that she wants to pleasure you in any way you want. She also guarantees complete anonymity. It is impossible that anyone would ever find out. Would you say yes? If so, it shows how much you value your freedom.

Now imagine that this same woman came and made the same offer, but this time she added that she would give you $10,000 in cash for letting her pleasure you. Would you say yes? Then that would be how much you value your freedom.

Perhaps she came once more, but this time she offered you $1 million to pleasure you. Would you say yes? If so, then that is how much you value your freedom.

So, at what price would you sell your freedom? Whatever number, if any, seems right, that number defines the value you place on your freedom.

God's Appraisal

The only way to walk in self-control is to view our freedom as priceless and invaluable, and to guard it with our lives. We must value our personal freedom above all else. Once we see the value of our freedom, we will not allow anything outside of us to control us. This will enable us to allow God's grace to pour into us and give us the strength not to give our control away to others.

Unfortunately, many believers do not value their freedom simply because they do not value themselves. Their minds have not been renewed to see themselves the way that God sees them. Much theology has reinforced a poor self-value among Christians, emphasizing our utter depravity and the deceitfulness of our hearts. Though it certainly is important to recognize our sinfulness in order to admit our need for a Savior and accept Jesus' sacrifice for our sins, this is not the standard for our existence *after* we have received new life in Christ. Paul creates a clear demarcation when he writes repeatedly that believers are now dead to sin and alive in Christ (see Rom. 6:11-13; Eph. 2:1-6; Col. 2:13). We are a new creation, and Father God has good things to say about us.

Consider this: God's value for you is so great that He purchased your freedom with the death of Jesus Christ. God is not a fool. He was not duped into overpaying for something of little value. God didn't take the most precious thing in Heaven (His Son) and trade it for a piece of trash. God defined your value when He paid for you, declaring that you are valued at the price of the death of the Son of God.

Jesus spelled this out for us in the simplest of terms, saying that God loves us *as much as* He loves Jesus! Jesus prayed, *"that the world may know that You sent Me, and loved them, even as You have loved Me"* (John 17:23 NASB). Like the mother who values the life of her children so much that she will die saving them, God gave us the ultimate value when He purchased our freedom from sin.

When we *get* this, we will understand that our freedom is the most priceless commodity in existence. Jesus gave everything for our freedom; shouldn't we do the same?

WHEN WE HATE OURSELVES

Unfortunately, most people who struggle in bondage to sin don't really understand their value. Deep inside they believe themselves to be unworthy of Christ's sacrifice. God says, "You are My treasure," and such people respond, "No, I'm just trash." By refusing to accept their God-proclaimed value, they are calling God either a fool or a liar. After all, if they truly are trash and Jesus still gave His life for them, then He is a fool. Though they do not consciously believe or confess this about Jesus, it is the logical conclusion and overflow of their attitude toward themselves. Because they do not believe in their personal value, they operate in self-destructive and self-rejecting behaviors and subconsciously sabotage their own success. This overflows into their relationships with others and their ability to live as powerful people.

Jesus subtly addressed this in His response to the question, "What is the greatest commandment?" He responded:

> The foremost is, "Hear, O Israel! The Lord our God is one Lord; and you shall love the Lord your God with all your heart, and with all your soul, and with all your mind, and with all your strength." The second is this, "**You shall love your neighbor as yourself.**" There is no other commandment greater than these (Mark 12:29-31 NASB).

What many people miss about this second commandment is that, in order to love their neighbors as themselves, they first must *love themselves*. If we do not love and value ourselves, which means understanding and accepting God's love and value for us, we will have no grid for how to love others. Jesus said we should love each other in the same way that He has loved us; He also said our distinguishing mark as His followers would be that we love one another (see John 13:34-35). But if we don't know *how much* He loves and values us, we won't know how to properly love others.

If we don't value ourselves, it is impossible for us to value others. That is how a cycle of devaluing happens. For a man to feel valuable and powerful, he devalues women in pornography for a temporary power "fix." He steals value from her to feed his deficit. The more powerless he feels, the farther he must go for his "fix." Thus pornography eventually fails to meet the need, and strip clubs come next, followed perhaps by escort services. Thus the downward cycle progresses, all because a powerless person is trying to feel powerful.

PEOPLE OF VALUE SET BOUNDARIES

When we have a revelation of our value, we establish personal boundaries to protect and communicate that value. As Danny Silk so aptly illustrates:

> Boundaries communicate value for what is inside of those boundaries. If you have several junk cars out in a field, it's called an eyesore. If you put a fence around those cars, then you have a wrecking yard. And, if you put a building around those cars, you have a garage. With each increase of limits, you increase the value of what is inside. When you raise the level of what you require before you will allow access, you increase the value of what you have. To all who are near, we send a clear message about the level of value we have for ourselves by the way we establish boundaries.[2]

Proverbs 25:28 says, *"Like a city whose walls are broken through is a person who lacks self-control."* We see this throughout society. The greater value a thing or person has, the greater the security. Thus, presidents and government officials ride in armored vehicles while normal people ride in normal cars. Large sums of money and other valuables are kept in bank vaults, while small sums of money are kept in wallets. A bank without walls would not be a bank, but a free-for-all that would quickly turn into anarchy. This is true of our inner world as well.

We can learn much about boundaries from the Book of Nehemiah. Nehemiah, a Jew living in exile, heard that the city of Jerusalem had no walls to protect it and was, therefore, regularly robbed (see Neh. 1:3). It grieved Nehemiah that God's city would be unprotected and prey to thieves—that it would be held in such low esteem.

Because of this, he asked the king to allow him to return to Jerusalem in order to rebuild the wall, which he did. Once in Jerusalem, Nehemiah inspected the broken walls and called the people living there to build with him. His words to them demonstrate the connection between a lack of boundaries and a lack of value: *"Come, let us rebuild the wall of Jerusalem so that we will no longer be a reproach"* (Neh. 2:17 NASB).

The book chronicles their struggle to rebuild the walls while also fighting off the attacks of neighbors who did not want the walls in place. Though some of these men did everything they could to control, manipulate, and intimidate Nehemiah into giving up, Nehemiah stood strong. When threatened, he did not respond in fear. When the enemy asked to meet with him, Nehemiah declined, saying that he had important work to do and could not leave (see Neh. 6:1-12). When he was told of a plot against his life, Nehemiah responded, *"Should a man like me flee? And could one such as I go into the temple to save his life? I will not go in"* (Neh. 6:11 NASB).

Here we find the key to Nehemiah's self-control; he knew who he was and he understood his value. He provides an excellent example of someone who was powerful and who was able to complete his goal, because his value was settled and his personal boundaries were, therefore, maintained.

PARAMETERS AND HOT DOGS

As Nehemiah demonstrates, powerful boundaries are important because they reinforce our value to other people. Yet not all boundaries are healthy (as most of us have observed in the lives of people we know). Based on the four communication styles we discussed in the last chapter, we can see that there are essentially two ways in which powerless people handle boundaries: passively and aggressively.

Aggressive people have mile-high barbed wire security boundaries around their hearts; based on fear, they indiscriminately exclude everyone from their inner lives (as we discussed earlier). The opposite approach manifests in passive people who lack boundaries and allow others to control them. Such people have done an excellent job communicating the fact that they don't value themselves; thus, others treat them with disrespect. Clearly, neither of these demonstrates healthy, powerful communication.

The healthy approach to boundaries is found in the Assertive communication style, which values both self and others. While passive people disrespect themselves (a lack of boundaries) and aggressive people disrespect others (extreme boundaries), assertive people respect both themselves and others by creating boundaries that facilitate healthy interaction. Because of these boundaries, no one plays control games, and genuine vulnerability and connection are fostered.

The Assertive communication style works well when both people are committed to it, but what happens when an assertive person dialogues with someone living in one of the unhealthy and powerless communication styles?

That is when the value of healthy boundaries comes into focus. One helpful definition of the word *boundaries* could be "parameters," which carries with it the connotation of "knowing your limits." People of self-control know their personal parameters, the constraints in which they have chosen to operate. They have chosen them based on righteousness and personal preference. These parameters cannot be moved or crossed, but they also are not going to electrocute anyone who touches them.

For example, imagine you, as a powerful man, have decided that you do not like and never want to eat hot dogs. However, one day you're grilling with a good buddy, and he whips out a pack of hot dogs and begins to pressure you into eating one. He knows you don't like them, but he has decided that he wants to strong-arm you into eating one as a joke. He's not trying to be malicious, but because of his lack of self-control and respect, he is attempting to violate your boundaries and undermine your powerfulness.

So how would you respond? Would you passively give in and eat one, even while inside you feel resentful, violated, and powerless? Or perhaps you would aggressively react, belligerently standing your ground and saying something like, "Man, leave me alone. You're always trying to tell me what to do."

If your buddy is an aggressive person, such an exchange could escalate into yelling or scuffling or storming away. Though in this scenario you hold your ground about the hot dogs, you still react in a powerless way by allowing your buddy to control your emotional response—and you disrespect him through accusation.

Rather, the powerful response would sound something like, "Hey, man, I don't eat hot dogs. You're welcome to eat one if you'd like. I, however, am aiming for that big, juicy steak."

Notice here that you don't tell your buddy what to do ("leave me alone") or blame-shift ("you're always telling me what to do"). You simply tell him what you are doing and what you are not doing, which communicates that you are in control of yourself and you know it. If your buddy persists in harassing you, as a powerful man you will kindly tell him that he can drop it and stay, or he can take his hot dogs elsewhere.

Situations like this help you analyze what level of connection you want to have with certain people and how high your walls need to be around them. The more persistently people try to violate your self-control, the higher your walls are. But it is important to distinguish that these walls are not an excuse to be rude or to lash out in anger. Your walls are for the purpose of telling other people what you will do; they are not for the purpose of telling them what they should do or what's wrong with them. Your boundaries protect your self-control and prevent destructive people from entering your inner world, while also providing an environment for healthy relationships.

Jesus demonstrated this in His earthly relationships. Though He loved everyone and treated everyone with respect, He maintained various levels of relationship with different groups of people. John, "the disciple Jesus loved," was His closest friend (see John 13:23). Peter and James joined John as members of Jesus' inner circle (see Matt. 17:1; Mark 5:37; 14:33). Next were the 12 disciples, then the 70 whom He commissioned in ministry (see Luke 10:1-12), and then the 120 who faithfully followed Him during His ministry, becoming the first members of the Church after Pentecost (see Acts 1:15).

Jesus' exchange with His followers after the return to the 70 clearly demonstrates this dynamic.

> *The seventy returned with joy, saying, "Lord, even the demons are subject to us in Your name." And He said to them, "I was watching Satan fall from heaven like lightning...."*
>
> *At that very time He rejoiced greatly in the Holy Spirit, and said, "I praise You, O Father, Lord of heaven and earth, that You have hidden these things from the wise and intelligent and have revealed them to infants. Yes, Father, for this way was well-pleasing in Your sight. All things have been handed over to Me by My Father, and no one knows who the Son is*

except the Father, and who the Father is except the Son, **and anyone to whom the Son wills to reveal Him."**

Turning to the disciples, He said privately, *"Blessed are the eyes which see the things you see, for I say to you, that many prophets and kings wished to see the things which you see, and did not see them, and to hear the things which you hear, and did not hear them"* (Luke 10:17-18;21-24 NASB).

I want to highlight two aspects of this passage. First, Jesus said that He gets to choose those to whom He will reveal the nature and character of God. From this we can conclude that the more intimately we know Jesus, the more He shares with us. We are all invited into relationship with God, but not all of us are privy to His secrets.[3]

Second, in the midst of teaching the 70, Jesus pulled aside the 12 to privately share something with them that He did not choose to share with the whole group. Jesus was assertive enough to set boundaries, which is how powerful people maintain value for themselves.

PEOPLE OF VALUE SAY NO

Another crucial aspect of boundary-setting is the ability to say no to other people's demands. This doesn't mean that you can never change your mind or do a favor for someone else. What I'm talking about is when everything in you wants to say no to the request. You may even have pressing reasons why you cannot fulfill the request. But instead of simply saying, "I'm sorry, but I can't do that for you," you agree to do it simply out of fear.

If you can't say no, it's evidence that you do not value yourself. You fear the rejection or anger that might come at you if you say no, and you believe that your desires and your ability to choose don't matter as much as the other person's.

Those who are driven by fear and don't value themselves enough to say no end up living powerless lives.

Joseph Versus Samson

The Bible provides us with two examples which show the difference between a man who could say no (Joseph) and a man who couldn't (Samson). Both of these men faced sexual temptation. Both had a significant call of God and the anointing to bring deliverance to a nation, yet their responses to temptation absolutely determined their success.

Let's look at Joseph first. Joseph had a dream about his destiny, but he did not fully understand it, and in his immaturity, he bragged about it to his brothers. In response, they sold him into slavery in Egypt (see Gen. 37). This could have been demoralizing for Joseph; it could have caused him to feel powerless and to lose his sense of identity and value. However, his response to temptation was just the opposite:

> *...Now Joseph was handsome in form and appearance. It came about after these events that his master's wife looked with desire at Joseph, and she said, "Lie with me." But he refused and said to his master's wife, "Behold, with me here, my master does not concern himself with anything in the house, and he has put all that he owns in my charge. There is no one greater in this house than I, and he has withheld nothing from me except you, because you are his wife. How then could I do this great evil and sin against God?" As she spoke to Joseph day after day, he did not listen to her to lie beside her or be with her. Now it happened one day that he went into the house to do his work, and none of the men of the household was there inside. She caught him by his garment, saying, "Lie with me!" And he left his garment in her hand and fled, and went outside (Genesis 39:6-12 NASB).*

Joseph's ability to say no in this very tempting situation demonstrates his sense of value. Notice Joseph's emphasis on his personal responsibility, both to his earthly master and to God. This shows his understanding of his own power of self-control; though he had been enslaved and was in a sense outwardly powerless, internally he knew that he was still the master of his own fate. And as a powerful man, he chose to align his choices with righteousness. He still knew who he was and who he was called to be; therefore, he maintained his boundaries zealously. Though the immediate result of his integrity was being falsely accused and sent to prison, his choice prepared him to receive his breakthrough and become the deliverer of Egypt, Israel, and the entire region during the famine.

Conversely, Samson did not have boundaries. Though he had massive supernatural anointing, he couldn't walk with character due to his inability to say no. Samson was physically very powerful, yet he was inwardly powerless. He did not value himself or his anointing and, therefore, felt no reluctance in giving control of himself to a series of women.

Samson did not have the boundaries in place to enable him to withstand temptation. First he married a Philistine woman, even though the Philistines were the enemies of Israel that God had called Samson to defeat (see Judg. 14). Samson ended up losing his wife in a disagreement with the Philistines. He later turned to a prostitute, and finally fell in love with the famous Delilah, who used his inability to say no for her own gain (see Judg. 16:1-21).

Seeing Samson's "addiction" to Delilah, the Philistines offered her money to find the source of his strength. When she began badgering Samson about it, his weakness was revealed by his response: instead of just saying, "It's none of your business," he lied to her repeatedly and stayed with her, even though her manipulation was glaringly obvious.

The Bible's commentary on this event is very interesting: *"It came about when she pressed him daily with her words and urged him, that his soul was annoyed to death"* (Judg. 16:16 NASB). Because of Samson's lack of boundaries, he allowed himself to be worn down to the point of compromise.

Both Samson and Joseph dealt with women who persistently pressed them to do wrong. Joseph responded by assertively saying no and eventually fleeing. Samson foolishly tried to evade being questioned. He used deceit and ignored Delilah's obvious ill intentions, wrongly assuming that he could not be overcome. Eventually, Delilah wore him down; and even though she had betrayed him before, he trusted her with his secret. As a result, his eyes were gouged out and he was placed in forced labor. Unlike Joseph, Samson did not have the inner strength to say no. Though a physically powerful man, he was not truly powerful because he didn't value himself enough to set boundaries.

As we can see in the lives of Samson and Joseph, supernatural anointing has nothing to do with character. Operating in the supernatural is not an indicator of emotional and spiritual health. The supernatural operates merely by faith, as Paul wrote in Galatians 3:5: *"So again I ask, does God give you His Spirit and work miracles among you by the works of the law, or by your believing what you heard?"*

All we have to do is look at history to see many greatly anointed men of God who fell into sin, whether sexual sin or something else, despite their gifts and calling. This is the point of First Corinthians 13:

> *If I **speak with the tongues of men and of angels**, but do not have love, I have become a noisy gong or a clanging cymbal. If I **have the gift of prophecy**, and **know all mysteries and all knowledge**; and if I **have all faith, so as to remove mountains**, but do not have love, I am nothing. And if I **give all my possessions to feed the poor**, and if I **surrender my body to be burned**, but do not have love, it profits me nothing* (1 Corinthians 13:1-3 NASB).

People who possess the impressive manifestations of the anointing that Paul lists here usually gain a measure of leadership and influence in the Church. However, many have ended up like Samson (rather than Joseph) because they do the right things, but not from love. Walking in love toward others requires that we love and value ourselves (see Mark 12:30-31). Bottom line: If we see that we are valuable, we will use appropriate boundaries, and the power of *no* will help to protect our value.

PEOPLE OF VALUE ARE PEOPLE OF REST

Those who value themselves not only say no and set boundaries, but they also maintain a heart of *rest*. As we discussed earlier, knowing our value is primarily connected to knowing God and the way He sees us. When we understand His unconditional affection for us, we can cease from striving for approval and simply rest in our identity in Him. Like Mary, we are able to rest from our works and receive from His presence (see Luke 10:38-42).

In Hebrews chapter 4, there is a long passage about entering God's rest—I would like to share one insight from this passage.

> *There remains, then, a Sabbath-rest for the people of God; for anyone who enters God's rest also rests from their works, just as God did from His. Let us, therefore, **make every effort to enter that rest**, so that no one will perish by following their example of disobedience* (Hebrews 4:9-11).

In our pre-Christian days, we didn't have to work at sinning; it came naturally. A sinful lifestyle simply flowed out of us effortlessly. You could say that we were at rest in the sinful nature. Now that we have been given the new nature and have been made "new creations," we need to enter into the place of rest in our new identity. It might take some work at first, but Hebrews 4:9-11 says, in essence, that we are to work to come into a place of rest in God, as contrasted with how we used to be at rest in sin.

Throughout the Bible we can see that God has always been trying to get us to rest in Him. Let us find examples by looking more closely at His interactions with Adam, Noah, Moses, Jesus, and the apostle John.

ADAM

In the first five days of creation, God made the heavens and the Earth. On the sixth day, He created Adam and commissioned him, saying,

> *Be fruitful and multiply, and fill the earth, and subdue it; and rule over the fish of the sea and over the birds of the sky and over every living thing that moves on the earth* (Genesis 1:28 NASB).

Adam didn't start working right away, however. Instead, his first day on Earth consisted of spending the seventh day of creation resting with God. Rest was the first thing that Adam learned about his Creator. Adam was to work *from* a place of rest—rest *then* work, not work until tired and then rest.

Notice the sequence described for each day of creation: *"And there was evening and there was morning..."* (Gen. 1:5,8,13,19,23,31). The reason that night comes before day is that, in God's economy, rest comes before work, night comes before day, and sleep comes before activity.

The first revelation that Adam received about God was that rest is the foundation of relationship with Him (see Gen. 1:31–2:2). The writer of Hebrews explained that *"the one who has entered His rest has himself also rested from his works, as God did from His"* (Heb. 4:10 NASB).

If we properly value ourselves, we will learn to put rest before work and find security in our identity in God *first*. From that position, we can begin to fulfill our destinies. People who still struggle with knowing their value tend to derive worth from their work; thus they end up striving.

NOAH

Even when God remodeled the planet with the flood, He provided the ark as a picture of resting in the storm. After the flood, the ark came to rest on a mountaintop, and a dove was sent out to find a resting place (see Gen. 8:8-12). This is a beautiful picture of how we must learn to rest *through* the storm and *after* the storm.

In the New Testament we find that Jesus modeled a lifestyle of rest by falling asleep in the boat during a severe storm (see Matt. 8:24-26). This is the standard for our lives. In Christ, there is rest in every storm. The storm was so bad that the waves were actually crashing over the boat. The disciples were terrified, believing they might die. (And they were experienced fishermen, no less!) However, when they awoke Jesus, He rebuked them for their fear and lack of faith. The fact that Jesus actually *rebuked* the disciples in this situation shows that this sort of rest in the storm is mandatory in the life of a believer.

MOSES

As Adam learned, the first way of knowing God and His ways is to know His rest. Centuries later, Moses asked two things of God: "Who will go with us?" and "Show me Your ways" (see Exod. 33:12-13).

The Lord replied, *"My presence shall go with you, and I will give you rest"* (Exod. 33:14 NASB). In other words, God's answer to "Show me Your ways" was "I will give you rest."

All revelation of the ways of God sits on the foundation of rest. Even when God gave Moses the Ten Commandments, He was teaching Moses His ways. The first three commandments show humankind how to interact with God: we are not to worship other gods, have idols, or take His name in vain. The last six commandments teach us how to treat each other: we must honor our parents and must not murder, commit adultery, steal, lie, or covet. The fourth commandment shows us how to treat ourselves: we are to keep the Sabbath.

> *Remember the sabbath day, to keep it holy. Six days you shall labor and do all your work, but the seventh day is a sabbath of the Lord your God; in it you shall not do any work...* (Exodus 20:8-10 NASB).

Between the discussion of our relationship with God and our relationships with others is the one command about how we are to treat ourselves correctly. As Jesus said, *"The Sabbath was made for man, and not man for the Sabbath"* (Mark 2:27 NASB).

The Sabbath is not about keeping another rule; it's about personal health and valuing ourselves. God knows we need rest, physically as well as emotionally and spiritually. More than that, God believes we are worthy of having a rest. He values us enough to say, "Take a break" (see Mark 6:30-32).

Child labor laws exist to prevent children from being exploited in working environments. These laws were created because factory owners did not value children properly and, therefore, did not give them the rest their bodies needed—not to mention the freedom to play and enjoy childhood. The Sabbath is our "child labor law," because in it God is saying, "I value you too much to overwork you."

God also knows that safeguarding this place of rest in our lives is the crux to enabling healthy relationship with Him and others. This is why He includes rest in His Top Ten. Not resting is likened to committing murder or adultery, because it is connected to our ability to live out the rest of the commands. Rest is that important in our lives.

If we hold God in His proper place of esteem (commands 1-3), and we rest with Him (command 4), then we will value ourselves and be able to treat others appropriately (commands 5-10).

JESUS

In the same way that Adam's first interaction with God was to learn about rest, our first interaction with Jesus involves rest. When Jesus calls for us to come into relationship with Him, His first offer is *rest:*

> *Come to Me, all you who are weary and burdened, and I will give you rest. Take My yoke upon you and learn from Me, for I am gentle and humble in heart, and you will find rest for your souls. For My yoke is easy and My burden is light* (Matthew 11:28-30).

Just prior to this verse, Jesus says that being childlike is essential to knowing the ways of God and that He reveals the Father to whomever He wishes (see Matt. 11:25-27). Then He invites us to come and find rest in Him. From this, we can see that rest, which is childlike faith in Jesus, brings us into a place of intimacy with God the Father. Relationship comes not through striving in our own worthiness, but through resting in His.

JOHN

The apostle John, who was most likely Jesus' closest friend during His time on Earth, wrote, *"This is how we know that we belong to the truth and how we set our hearts at rest in His presence"* (1 John 3:19).

As believers, it is our choice and responsibility to maintain hearts that are full of peace and rest, not anxiety, fear, or stress. Even in the worst of situations we can say, *"You prepare a table before me in the presence of my enemies...."* (Ps. 23:5).

King David was regularly put in rough situations where he had to choose to *set his heart at rest.* Typically, when we are in the midst of the enemy's camp and are surrounded, the Lord prepares a feast of revelation for us—*if* we remain at rest.

Consider how God sent Gideon into the enemy's camp in the middle of the night to hear a prophetic word (see Judg. 7:9-15). This is a clear example of how God prepares a table in the presence of our enemies. If we can learn to keep our hearts at rest in any situation, we will stay connected to His presence and be able to maintain an appropriate sense of value for ourselves and others.

REST RESTORES WHOLENESS

As we discussed previously, because of the lies we've believed, many of us men have fallen into hopelessness and powerlessness. Without boundaries and the ability to say no, many have failed to protect their value. If this is true of you, then like a city without walls, you likely need to be restored to wholeness.

Our wholeness is restored in the place of rest in Jesus. The Bible says, *"...In returning and rest you shall be saved* [made whole]..." (Isa. 30:15 NKJV). Returning requires coming back to the foundation, which is resting in Christ (see Matt. 11:28-30). We must always start over from rest. Then *"quietness and confidence shall be* [our] *strength"* (Isa. 30:15b NKJV).

We find wholeness and healing not in striving to be better people or stirring our own righteousness, but in resting in Christ's work on the cross. He has already purchased our freedom for us; He has made us *powerful* and *valuable*. We simply need to rest in our new identity.

Tool 1

List your answers to the following question: In the past, where has my value come from?

Now write a second list, answering this question: Where should my value come from for the future?

Tool 2

Now, let's create a ladder to help answer the following questions: What are my boundaries? and, When do I say no?

Begin by drawing a simple picture of a ladder. On the top rung write God's name; on the second rung write your spouse's name; on the third rung write your children's names. For the fourth and subsequent lower rungs, you will have to prayerfully consider your other relationships to determine who goes on each rung. Make sure you complete your ladder by considering your occupation, co-workers, extended family, friends, etc.

This is an exercise to help you map out your relationships, priorities, and boundary levels. Next, write a number next to each rung. God 1, Spouse 2, Children 3, and so on. If you discover that someone on the sixth rung is trying to take the time and attention that rightfully belongs to a fourth-rung individual, you must assertively communicate your boundaries to that person.

When you address such issues, it is important for the people involved to feel loved and valued, and not rejected by you. Take care also not to push people down to even lower rungs as a way to punish them or to self-protect out of fear. Simply be powerful and assertive and place them back at the levels where they belong.

Over time you will see relationships shift from level to level. This is perfectly healthy and natural; some will grow closer to you and some will recede to lower rungs. Be careful never to change the order of the top three rungs; if you do, your life will become unhealthy.

Tool 3

Resting with God is the foundation of your relationship with Him (not your works). Starting today, take a few minutes each day to close your eyes, sit back, and fellowship with Him in your heart. Thank Him for all the wonderful things He has done for you. Thank Him for valuing you. Let Him speak into your heart the words of love and encouragement that you need to hear each day.

CHAPTER 4

YOU ARE NOT YOUR ACTIONS

*To be free is not merely to cast off one's chains, but to live
in a way that respects and enhances the freedom of others.*
—NELSON MANDELA

Slavery in the United States was abolished by the 13th Amendment on December 18th, 1865. How many slaves were there on December 19th? In reality, none, but many still lived like slaves. Many did because they never learned the truth; others knew and even believed that they were free, but chose to live as they had been taught.

Several plantation owners were devastated by this proclamation of emancipation. "We're ruined! Slavery has been abolished. We've lost the battle to keep our slaves."

But their chief spokesman slyly responded, "Not necessarily, as long as these people think they're still slaves, the proclamation of emancipation will have no practical effect. We don't have a legal right over them anymore, but many of them don't know it. Keep your slaves from learning the truth, and your control over them will not even be challenged."

"But, what if the news spreads?"

"Don't panic. We have another barrel in our gun. We may not be able to keep them from hearing the news, but we can still keep them from understanding it. They don't call me the father of lies for nothing. We still have the potential to deceive the whole world. Just tell them that they misunderstood the 13th Amendment. Tell them that they are going to be free, not that they are free already. The truth they heard is just positional truth, not actual truth. Someday they may receive the benefits, but not now."

"But, they'll expect me to say that. They won't believe me."

"Then pick out a few persuasive ones who are convinced that they're still slaves and let them do the talking for you. Remember, most of these free people were born as slaves and lived like slaves. All we have to do is to deceive them so that they still think like slaves. As long as they continue to do what slaves do, it will not be hard to convince them that they must still be slaves. They will maintain their slave identity because of the things they do.

The moment they try to profess that they are no longer slaves, just whisper in their ear, 'How can you even think you are no longer a slave when you are still doing things that slaves do?' After all, we have the capacity to accuse the brethren day and night."

Years later, many have still not heard the wonderful news that they have been freed, so naturally they continue to live the way they have always lived. Some have heard the good news, but evaluated it by what they are presently doing and feeling. They reason, "I'm still living in bondage, doing the same things I have always done. My experience tells me that

I must not be free. I'm feeling the same way I was before the proclamation, so it must not be true. After all, your feelings always tell the truth." So they continue to live according to how they feel, not wanting to be hypocrites!

One former slave hears the good news, and receives it with great joy. He checks out the validity of the proclamation, and finds out that the highest of all authorities has originated the decree. Not only that, but it personally cost the authority a tremendous price which He willingly paid, so that he could be free. His life is transformed. He correctly reasons that it would be hypocritical to believe his feelings and not believe the truth. Determined to live by what he knows to be true, his experiences began to change rather dramatically. He realizes that his old master has no authority over him and does not need to be obeyed. He gladly serves the one who set him free.[1]

Jesus acquired complete freedom for us at the cross, yet the devil has used many lies to keep us from receiving this freedom in full. The main area that the devil lies to us about is our identity. If we do not understand the truth of what was accomplished for us, then we cannot receive it in full. The battle for sexual purity is a battle rooted in our identity.

The Bible tells us that *"as* [a man] *thinks in his heart, so is he"* (Prov. 23:7 NKJV). This obviously has limitations. Just because you think you can fly doesn't mean that you can! But within these limitations, we find that Jesus has given us power over sin and the devil. If a man *"thinks in his heart"* that he is free from sexual bondage, then *so is he*! The war for sexual purity will be won because we are set free by believing the truth (see John 8:32).

The clinical approach to sexual sin has labeled lust as a disease, and those who have it are called sexual addicts. Those who follow this approach say, "Once an addict, always an addict." Biblically, I cannot agree with this statement. You may *have been* a sexual addict, but you *are now* the righteousness of God in Christ Jesus (see 1 Cor. 1:30). You may even still be acting like a sexual addict, but that is merely because you have not realized that your identity has changed. You have a new identity, and you must receive a revelation of who you are now. Many Christians continue to walk in sin after salvation because they don't realize who they are now. If they truly realized who they have become in Christ, then they would be set free.

We must come to understand that, regarding the battle of sexual sin, *we are not the problem. Rather, what we believe about ourselves is the problem.* We will only find freedom when we believe what God believes about us.

As I stated earlier, most people form their identity from their actions. Many people have said, "I am a sinner saved by grace." This is a massive theological error. Once you accept Christ, you are no longer a sinner. God considers you now to be a saint. Yet because people continue to choose sin at times, they consider themselves to still be sinners. *In essence, such people are sinning by faith.* They believe themselves to be sinners; therefore, they sin. If they believed God's Word, which says that they are righteous, then they would walk as righteous people.

Our identity is not the sum of our actions; identity is the foundation from which our actions flow. Thus, identity always precedes actions.

In Christ we have been made into the righteousness of God (see 1 Cor. 1:30; Rom. 5:17); that is our true identity. Once we understand this, our actions will flow forth from this truth. "I am the righteousness of God in Christ; therefore, I live and act righteously, because that is who I am!" Otherwise we will continue to view our actions and make statements like, "I keep sinning; therefore, I must still be a sinner." God changed our identities and put us into Christ so that our actions would flow out of our new identity in Him.

Our New Identity

In Genesis 1, we find that humankind was created in the image and likeness of God.

> *Then God said, "Let us make mankind **in Our image, in Our likeness**, so that they may rule over the fish in the sea and the birds in the sky, over the livestock and all the wild animals, and over all the creatures that move along the ground." **So God created mankind in His own image, in the image of God He created them;** male and female He created them* (Genesis 1:26-27).

Here we see that humankind didn't have to *do* anything to be like God; our identity already was "like God." However, the serpent introduced a lie stating that humankind must *do* something in order to *be* like God.

> *"You will not certainly die," the serpent said to the woman. "For God knows that when you eat from it your eyes will be opened, and you will be like God..."* (Genesis 3:4-5).

Many have misread this temptation and thought that Eve was tempted by the opportunity of being like God. That interpretation makes no sense, however, because Eve was already like God. She didn't have to do anything more to be like Him; she had been created in His image. The serpent lied to her by saying that her identity, her "God-likeness," would come about through her actions. The serpent actually deceived Eve into thinking that her actions were able to determine her identity. Eve should have stood firm in her identity, but instead she forgot who she was.

> *And Jehovah God saith to the woman, "What [is] this thou hast done?" and the woman saith, **"The serpent hath caused me to forget--and I do eat"*** (Genesis 3:13 YLT).

With God, identity always precedes actions. That is why God created us in His likeness and His image, so that out of our identity would flow actions that reflect Him. Eve was the first one to believe the lie that she wasn't like God and that she had to *do* something to try to be like God. Humankind was not meant to strive and perform to act like God. Eve was created like God, and if she hadn't forgotten who she was, she would have naturally continued to be like God without even trying!

We must return to seeing ourselves the way God sees us. Remember: *We will only find freedom when we believe what God believes about us.* Renewing the mind transforms us because we begin to see ourselves the way that God sees us, and that corrected identity changes our lives. We must grasp what God declares our identity to be; then our actions will flow from that place of understanding.

Let's examine four points of view regarding identity. There is:

1. The way that the devil, the accuser of the brethren, sees us.

2. The way that others see us.

3. The way that we choose to see ourselves.

4. The way that God sees us.

When we agree with the devil's opinion of us, we end up living as defeated, bitter, and condemned people. When we try to live according to the way that others see us, we live insecure lives filled with the fear of people. When we live according to how we see ourselves, we constantly tally up the sum of our actions to determine what kind of people we are.

None of these perspectives give us a proper understanding of our identity. Rather, I suggest that the only healthy identity is seeing ourselves the way that God sees us. Our minds are renewed when we come into agreement with God's point of view.

Although you might observe your ongoing sin and try to equate this to your identity ("I sin; therefore, I am a sinner"), God sees your identity first ("You are a saint; therefore, you should sin no longer"). According to God, actions do not add up to your identity; your identity determines your actions. That is why He paid such a high price to give you a new identity, to put you into Christ, and to make you righteous. *Even when you mess up,* God sees you according to your identity.

It was when humankind was at its absolute worst and most depraved, when God hadn't even spoken to Israel for 400 years, that He chose to send Jesus to Earth. God didn't wait until people were acting in a manner worthy of His sacrifice. No. He sent Jesus because people were not living up to their identity; because of sin they had fallen out of step with who they really were. So Jesus came to re-establish that identity. God always sees the inherent worth and value of people, despite all the sin and trash.

Our actions do not equate our identity or our value to God. Because we were created in His image and because He calls us His own, He is the one who knows who we truly are! We are His children, and our identity does not change because of our failures. As John wrote: *"See what great love the Father has lavished on us, that we should be called children of God! And that is what we are!..."* (1 John 3:1).

We see in the examples of Gideon, Sarah, and Moses, that God doesn't equate our actions with our identity. Instead, God always focuses on our true identity and value, which are found in Him and the destinies He created us to fulfill.

GIDEON

When the angel of the Lord appeared to Gideon, he was simply a coward hiding from Israel's enemies and threshing wheat in a winepress. Yet the angel declared that Gideon was a *"mighty man of valor"* (Judg. 6:12 NKJV).

This is exactly how God interacts with us. God says things like, "You are a mighty man, a pure man, a holy man, and a righteous man!" Even though our actions might state otherwise, God declares those things to be true of us because that is who He made us to be. Gideon, like many of us, began to argue with God because he was convinced that, based on his cowardly actions, he must be a coward. Many of us have told God that He is wrong because we tend to focus on our actions and not our identity (see Judg. 6).

SARAH

When the Lord told Abraham and Sarah that they would have a child in their old age, Sarah laughed mockingly at God! Yet the Lord records the story in Hebrews 11:11 saying that *"by faith even Sarah, who was past childbearing age, was enabled to bear children because she considered Him faithful who had made the promise."*

Here we can see that God looks beyond our sin and foolish actions, and He sees us very differently. From a natural standpoint, no one would read the story of Sarah laughing at God and come to the conclusion that she had great faith. Yet that is what God wrote in Hebrews 11:11. God's point of view is not determined by our actions. He is our loving Creator, and no wrong actions are going to change our identity in His eyes.

MOSES

Moses, at 40 years of age, had to flee his cushy life in the palace and live in the wilderness because he had murdered an Egyptian. Moses was a fugitive murderer! Yet again, God's point of view was quite different:

> *By faith Moses, when he had grown up, refused to be known as the son of Pharaoh's daughter. He chose to be mistreated along with the people of God rather than to enjoy the fleeting pleasures of sin* (Hebrews 11:24-25).

Moses' actions defined him as a murderer, yet God declared him to be a deliverer; and because he chose to believe God's version of his identity, Moses was able to become a mighty deliverer.

The conflict between how Moses, Gideon, and Sarah acted and how God viewed them is the same conflict that we are dealing with. *We must stop focusing on our actions in our struggle to figure out our identity.* We must find out from our Father and Creator what our true identity is, and then we must walk out our actions in accordance with that identity.

When God speaks, His goal is to align us with our true identity. When He comes to speak to a coward, He says, "I created you as a mighty man, I know who you are better than you do. Don't look at your feelings or actions; your self-assessment is wrong. I am God, and I established your identity. I know who you really are. You are a mighty man."

God tells us who we really are so that we can live from His point of view. Believing what He declares about our identity will cause new actions to flow out of us. As we begin to really know who we are in Him, we will act according to that belief.

When God spoke to Abram and Sarai (later to become Abraham and Sarah), who were barren, He told Abram, *"...I have made you a father of many nations"* (Gen. 17:5). The apostle Paul said that God *"...calleth those things which be not as though they were"* (Rom. 4:17 KJV). God is not looking at our present sinful actions to figure out who we are. God comes to tell us who we are so that new actions will flow out of our newly-recognized identity.

Confronting with Honor

It is very easy to focus on the wrong things. Much of the time we focus on actions and the outward flesh. That is exactly what Paul told us not to do; rather we are to be compelled by love, and we are to refuse to view people according to their flesh.

For the love of Christ compels us, because we judge thus: that if One died for all, then all died; and He died for all, that those who live should live no longer for themselves, but for Him who died for them and rose again.

Therefore, from now on, we regard no one according to the flesh. *Even though we have known Christ according to the flesh, yet now we know Him thus no longer. Therefore, if anyone is in Christ, he is a new creation; old things have passed away; behold, all things have become new* (2 Corinthians 5:14-17 NKJV).

This passage shows that we are not to view people through the lens of their actions and lifestyles, but according to the way that Christ views them. Christ always keeps His eye on a person's inherent value. He sees each one of us as someone who was worth His death.

When people have sin in their lives, it must be confronted, but the sin is not their identity. As the confronter, it is important to keep the "confrontee's" true identity as the focus. If confrontees become focused on their sin and their failure, then they *will not be empowered* to move in a new direction. Notice how the apostle Paul confronted sin in the Corinthian believers:

*Get rid of the old yeast, so that you may be a new unleavened batch—**as you really are.** For Christ, our Passover lamb, has been sacrificed* (1 Corinthians 5:7).

*Get rid of the old yeast so that you may be dough of a new kind; **for in fact you are free from corruption.*** *For our Passover Lamb has already been offered in sacrifice—even Christ* (1 Corinthians 5:7 WNT).

This is the principle of *confronting with honor.* We must confront sin through the lens of people's true identity. I would paraphrase what

Paul said this way: *"Hey Corinthian, get these sinful actions out of your life because that isn't who you are. Jesus has cleansed you, so it is time to stop living like a sinner. That isn't you!"*

As we read in Chapter 2, the film character Rocky Balboa confronted his son Robert, saying, "Cowards do that, and that ain't you! You are better than that!"[2] This is how God confronts us in our sin, and this is how we should confront each other. Sin is not the focus; reminding people of their identity in Christ is the true focus. Our actions are not our identity; our actions flow from our identity. Thus, we must understand our identity in Christ so that we will live like Christ.

One last thought on this topic comes from the author of *Culture of Honor,* Pastor Danny Silk:

> Putting on the cloak of shame and guilt is not only unbecoming for us as His [God's] sons and daughters; it is a trap of powerlessness. Reaching in and grabbing our people by their true identities is an act of love that will live on far longer than the sting of failure and consequences. People can see and think when their identity is clear of fear and shame.[3]

When people sin, we must not make sin our focus, we must point them back to their true identity. We must not regard anyone according to the flesh, including ourselves. Through the lens of our true identity in Christ, we will each be empowered to deal with the sinful actions in our lives. We will know how to choose righteousness because we will be living from the reality of what God says about us.

Tool

Picture in your mind your worst memory, specifically of a mistake that you made. Consider what others would label you because of that mistake (i.e., *drunk, adulterer, thief,* etc.)

Now separate your action from your identity, for example:

- Instead of *drunk: I got drunk.*

- Instead of a*dulterer: I committed adultery.*

- Instead of *thief: I stole.*

When you sin, your identity does not change. Regardless of what you have done, you are still the righteousness of God in Christ—*even though* you chose to get drunk, commit adultery, or steal.

Use this exercise to separate your actions from your identity. Maintain your true identity in the face of your mistakes. *Your actions do not change who you are in Him.*

CHAPTER 5

YOU ARE CRUCIFIED IN CHRIST

You are crucified with Christ and you can add nothing to what He accomplished at the cross. To even try to die more is to insult the work of Jesus.

—JONATHAN WELTON

There has been much confusion regarding how a believer walks in the spirit and not in the flesh. A majority of this confusion stems from communicating in unclear terminology. Before we can discuss what Jesus has accomplished on our behalf, we must lay a clear foundation for accurate communication. Here are four terms and concepts that must be understood:

1. *Soul* refers to one of the three components of human beings: the spirit, the soul, and the body (see 1 Thess. 5:23). I agree with the standard definition of the soul as the mind, will, and emotions.

2. *Soulish* or *soulical*. These are not biblical terms and I will not be using them. Typically when these terms are used, it is in the context of communicating certain Gnostic teachings, which the Church has adopted.

3. *Self* is the word that Jesus used when He referred to "denying self." *Self* is *not* synonymous with the "flesh" or the "soul." The word *self* is better understood as a person's "reputation."

4. *The flesh, fleshly, carnal, carnality, the old nature, and the old man.* These are synonymous terms which refer to the part of man which is drawn after and under the influence of sin.

Now that we have defined our terms, we will proceed to address them and their usages in the Word.

Fighting the Soul

The famous author, Watchman Nee, has caused a lot of confusion regarding these four definitions, especially by teaching that the flesh is comprised of a combination of the soul and the body (in contrast to the definitions given above). I will expound more on the vital importance of this subtle distinction below.

I personally am the biggest Watchman Nee fan I have ever met. I have a "Watchman Nee shelf" in my library, which contains every title that Nee ever published. I have twice read his seminal work, *The Spiritual Man*—694 pages of profoundly deep teaching written in the 1930s and translated from the Chinese. This book has influenced modern thought towards the soul more than any other. It is with all due respect that I must correct an error in Nee's approach.

His teaching states that the spirit of the believer has been perfected. In contrast, the *soul* and *body* are defined as "the flesh," which is evil.

Clearly stated, the flesh is fundamentally evil and the spirit is fundamentally perfect and holy. This teaching creates a never-ending interior struggle between the soul and the spirit. This inner struggle concept has become prevalent throughout much of the modern Church. Yet the Bible does not teach this and this is not an accurate definition of *the flesh.*

The idea that the spirit of a person is perfect while the person's soul/body comprise the evil flesh is a fundamentally flawed, erroneous teaching. The Bible does not even teach that we have perfected spirits or that our souls are evil. This concept has come from a misunderstanding of Hebrews 12:23:

> *But you have come to Mount Zion, to the city of the living God, the heavenly Jerusalem. You have come to thousands upon thousands of angels in joyful assembly, to the church of the firstborn, whose names are written in heaven. You have come to God, the Judge of all, to the spirits of the righteous made perfect, to Jesus the mediator of a new covenant, and to the sprinkled blood that speaks a better word than the blood of Abel* (Hebrews 12:22-24).

Notice that the context of the spirits of righteous men made perfect is in reference to those who are already in Heaven. It is not accurate to use this verse to claim that Jesus perfects the human spirit at salvation. These were the righteous men of Hebrews 11 who have died and gone on to Heaven before us.

Secondly, the Bible states that the spirit of a believer can still be defiled after salvation:

> *Therefore, having these promises, beloved, let us cleanse ourselves from all defilement of flesh and spirit, perfecting holiness in the fear of God* (2 Corinthians 7:1 NASB).

This contradicts the idea that the spirit of a believer is already perfected.

Regarding the soul, the Lord has never condemned the human soul as an evil thing. In fact, He made the human soul before the Fall of Man. Adam and Eve both had souls. If the human soul were inherently evil, it would not have existed in Eden. To equate the soul with the flesh is inaccurate. Consider that Jesus instructed us to love the Lord with all our heart, soul, mind and strength (see Mark 12:30). The word *spirit* isn't even on the list, and if the soul is equal to the flesh, how could we possibly love God with our evil flesh?

Since our flesh nature is not composed of the soul and the body, then what is the flesh? *The flesh* refers to a person's lower nature. This lower nature in Scripture is called *the carnal nature, the flesh, the old nature, the body of death,* and *the old man.* The flesh is the internal part of humankind that is inclined toward evil desires. The flesh operates in all three realms of the human design: the spirit, soul, and body; every human being has a portion that is inclined toward unhealthy appetites. This is *the flesh.*

As long as we continue to confuse the soul with the flesh, we will continue to fight our own soul as if it were our enemy. A wrong interpretation of the following verse has caused much of the confusion regarding this topic. Let's look at it with new eyes:

> *For the word of God is living and powerful, and sharper than any two-edged sword, piercing even to the division of **soul and spirit,** and of joints and marrow, and is a discerner of the thoughts and intents of the heart* (Hebrews 4:12 NKJV)

When we read this verse believing that our spirit is good and our soul is bad, we create a division within ourselves that looks like this:

Diagram One

This diagram represents the belief of dualism, the division of soul from spirit. Yet look at this verse again. It actually says that the Word of God divides the soul and spirit; it is not saying that the Word divides the soul from the spirit as if one is good and one is bad. The Word divides both the soul and the spirit. Reading this verse correctly shows that the Word of God divides both the soul and spirit, you can see that an accurate division looks like this:

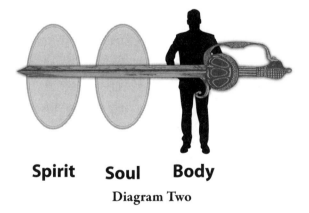

Spirit   Soul   Body

Diagram Two

The dividing sword pierces both the soul and the spirit. When you live according to the misinterpretation of diagram one, the spirit is placed in a lifelong battle against the soul. The Bible does not support the teaching of a good spirit and an evil soul; this concept is actually a Gnostic heresy of the first century.

During the early Church, the Gnostics taught that the spirit was good and the physical/emotional realms were evil, and therefore Jesus could not have come to Earth in an actual physical body. They taught that Jesus came to Earth only as an ethereal spirit-being. This teaching is heretical because it negates the truth of Jesus shedding His human blood for the remission of sin. The Gnostics gained so many followers in the early Church that John wrote his first epistle in response to their heresy.

> *That which was from the beginning, which we have heard, which we have **seen with our eyes, which we have looked at and our hands have touched**—this we proclaim concerning the Word of life. The life appeared; we have seen it and testify to it, and we proclaim to you the eternal life, which was with the Father and has appeared to us. We proclaim to you what we **have seen and heard**, so that you also may have fellowship with us. And our fellowship is with the Father and with His Son, Jesus Christ (1 John 1:1-3).*

John was writing to prove, as an eyewitness, that Jesus was not an ethereal ghost, but a real, physical person. John was the disciple who leaned his head upon Jesus' chest, and he knew that Jesus was not merely a spirit. He wrote saying that those who claim Jesus didn't have a physical body are actually anti-Christ.

> *Dear friends, do not believe every spirit, but test the spirits to see whether they are from God, because many false prophets have gone out into the world. This is how you can recognize the Spirit of God: Every spirit that **acknowledges that Jesus Christ has come in the flesh** is from God, but every spirit that does not acknowledge Jesus is not from God. This is the spirit of the antichrist, which you have heard is coming and even now is already in the world. (1 John 4:1-3).*

The ancient Gnostics, as well as Watchman Nee, taught according to Diagram One. (I am not saying that Nee was a Gnostic, but the Gnostics influenced his beliefs in this area.) This has led many modern Christians to believe that the soul and body are evil, but the Bible teaches nothing of the sort.

Actually, the body is referred to as the temple of the Holy Spirit (see 1 Cor. 3:16; 6:19), and the apostle Paul said that exercising the physical body is of value (see 1 Tim. 4:8).

The soul is never used in the Bible as a negative term. Typically, those who are influenced by Gnostic teaching refer negatively to things as being *soulish, of the soul, of the soul realm,* or as being related to *soul ties, soul power,* etc. But biblically speaking, there is nothing inherently evil about the soul. We are not in a battle against our own soul.

There is a struggle against the flesh, but the flesh is not the same as the soul. To follow the Gnostic heresy to its reasonable application, we must: 1) become completely spirit, 2) we must suppress our soul, or 3) we must pit the spirit against the soul for the rest of our lives. Thankfully, none of these options reflects biblical truth. Your soul is not the flesh and you never need to crucify your soul.

DENYING SELF

Many have been taught that *self* must be daily crucified and that *the self* is evil and must be denied. Although Jesus did say to deny *self,* the definition of *self* has been very convoluted. When Jesus referred to *self,* He was not talking about the soul. Also, He was not talking about the *self* as synonymous with *the flesh.* We know this because Jesus said to deny *self,* whereas the only answer for the flesh is crucifixion in Christ (see Gal. 2:20).

The best way to understand *self* is to define it as a person's *reputation.* Let's look again at what Jesus said regarding denying *self* with our new definition:

*Then He called the crowd to Him along with His disciples and said: "Whoever wants to be My disciple must **deny themselves** and take up their cross and follow Me. For whoever wants to save **their life** will lose it, but whoever loses **their life** for Me and for the gospel will save it"* (Mark 8:34-35).

*Then He said to them all: "Whoever wants to be My disciple must **deny themselves** and take up their cross daily and follow Me. For whoever wants to save **their life** will lose it, but whoever loses **their life** for Me will save it"* (Luke 9:23-24).

*Then Jesus said to His disciples, "Whoever wants to be My disciple must **deny themselves** and take up their cross and follow Me. For whoever wants to save **their life** will lose it, but whoever loses **their life** for Me will find it"* (Matthew 16:24-25).

It is clear in these passages that Jesus is talking to the nonbeliever and explaining how one becomes His follower. "Deny yourself" is something Jesus told those who were considering becoming His followers. He told them what it would cost them. The cost would be that they would lay down their lives and the control of their lives. This point is even clearer in Luke 14:

Large crowds were traveling with Jesus, and turning to them He said: "If anyone comes to Me and does not hate father and mother, wife and children, brothers and sisters—yes, even their own life—such a person cannot be My disciple. And whoever does not carry their cross and follow Me cannot be My disciple.

"Suppose one of you wants to build a tower. Won't you first sit down and estimate the cost to see if you have enough money to complete it? For if you lay the foundation and are not able to

finish it, everyone who sees it will ridicule you, saying, 'This person began to build and wasn't able to finish.'

"Or suppose a king is about to go to war against another king. Won't he first sit down and consider whether he is able with ten thousand men to oppose the one coming against him with twenty thousand? If he is not able, he will send a delegation while the other is still a long way off and will ask for terms of peace. In the same way, those of you who do not give up everything you have cannot be My disciples" (Luke 14:25-33).

Jesus spoke very plainly in these verses instructing His potential followers not to expect life to be easy. The first-century understanding of "taking up the cross" meant being willing to lay down one's reputation and be branded by society as a criminal. Jesus died a criminal's death on a criminal's cross and His followers had to count the cost of laying down their reputations to become rejects of society.

Jesus was *not* talking about how to win the battle against the flesh by applying His cross to your life. These sayings of Jesus have been grossly taken out of context to reinforce the Gnostic teachings referred to previously. The idea that Jesus was speaking theologically about how to daily crucify the flesh is not accurate.

OUR FLESH HAS BEEN CRUCIFIED

When Jesus died on the cross, He not only took our sinful actions upon Himself, He also took our flesh nature upon Himself. We have thereby been crucified with Christ.

*For Christ's love compels us, because we are convinced that one died for all, and **therefore all died**. And He died for all, that those who live should no longer live for themselves but for Him who died for them and was raised again* (2 Corinthians 5:14-15).

I have been crucified with Christ and I no longer live, but Christ lives in me. The life I now live in the body, I live by faith in the Son of God, who loved me and gave Himself for me (Galatians 2:20).

We live by faith that Jesus put our flesh to death on the cross by His crucifixion. This frees us from the control of the flesh and releases us to live a new life with a new nature. Romans chapter 6 goes much more in-depth regarding this transference from our flesh into the new nature of Jesus Christ.

Or don't you know that all of us who were baptized into Christ Jesus were baptized into His death? We were therefore buried with Him through baptism into death in order that, just as Christ was raised from the dead through the glory of the Father, we too may live a new life.

*For if we have been united with Him in a death like His, we will certainly also be united with Him in a resurrection like His. **For we know that our old self was crucified with Him so that the body ruled by sin might be done away with,** that we should no longer be slaves to sin—because anyone who has died has been set free from sin.*

*Now if **we died with Christ**, we believe that we will also live with Him. For we know that since Christ was raised from the dead, He cannot die again; death no longer has mastery over Him. The death He died, He died to sin once for all; but the life He lives, He lives to God.*

*In the same way, **count yourselves dead to sin** but alive to God in Christ Jesus* (Romans 6:3-11).

When Jesus died on the cross, our flesh was crucified with Him. When Jesus was resurrected, He released a new life and nature into

His followers. I say it this way: *Jesus died to deal with who you were, but was resurrected to make you into something new.*

Jesus came as the perfect sacrifice for sin. His death on the cross broke the power of every curse, provided forgiveness of sin, and put to death our sin nature. His death covered every sin once and for all time (see Heb. 9:28). His resurrection also accomplished something new. No previous sacrifice had ever been resurrected; every animal sacrifice of the Old Testament remained dead after its death. When Jesus arose, His resurrection gave us the power of a new nature and life!

IS OUR DEATH AN EVENT OR A PROCESS?

The majority of the Church believes that Jesus crucified our flesh, but that we also are in a process of crucifying our flesh. Yet, the Bible does not teach us to crucify ourselves. Our crucifixion in Christ is a past-tense, completely accomplished work. It is a past event, not a present process. We cannot add anything to what Christ has done for us.

Unfortunately, some Bible translations do not translate accurately the verb tenses regarding our crucifixion, but the original manuscripts of the New Testament are consistent: every verse regarding our crucifixion in Christ speaks of it as *past tense*, never *present* or *future*.

Here are some past-tense examples*:*

Those who belong to Christ Jesus **have crucified** *the flesh with its passions and desires* (Galatians 5:24).

In Him **you were** *also circumcised with a circumcision not performed by human hands. Your whole self ruled by the flesh* **was put off** *when* **you were** *circumcised by Christ...* (Colossians 2:11).

For you died, *and your life is now hidden with Christ in God* (Colossians 3:3).

*Therefore consider the members of your earthly body **as dead** to immorality, impurity, passion, evil desire, and greed, which amounts to idolatry* (Colossians 3:5 NASB).

*Do not lie to each other, **since you have taken off** your old self with its practices* (Colossians 3:9).

*Therefore, if anyone is in Christ, he is a new creation; **old things have passed away;** behold, all things have become new* (2 Corinthians 5:17 NKJV).

*But as for you, not in this manner did you learn the Christ, since, indeed, as is the case, you heard and in Him were taught just as truth is in Jesus, that **you have put off once for all** with reference to your former manner of life the old self who is being corrupted according to the passionate desires of deceit; moreover, that you are being constantly renewed with reference to the spirit of your mind; and that **you have put on once for all** the new self who after God was created in righteousness and holiness of truth* (Ephesians 4:20-24 Wuest).

*By no means! We are those **who have died** to sin; how can we live in it any longer? Or don't you know that all of us who **were baptized** into Christ Jesus **were baptized into His death**? We **were** therefore buried with Him through baptism into death in order that, just as Christ was raised from the dead through the glory of the Father, we too may live a new life.*

*For if we have been united with Him in a death like His, we will certainly also be united with Him in a resurrection like His. For we know that **our old self was crucified** with Him so that the body ruled by sin might be done away with, that* *we should no longer be slaves to sin—because anyone who has died **has been set free** from sin.*

*Now if we died with Christ, we believe that we will also live with Him. For we know that since Christ was raised from the dead, He cannot die again [neither can we!]; **death no longer has mastery** over Him. The death He died, He died to sin once for all; but the life He lives, He lives to God. In the same way, count yourselves **dead to sin** but alive to God in Christ Jesus.*

*You **have been** set free from sin and have become slaves to righteousness* (Romans 6:2-11).

*So, my brothers and sisters, **you also died** to the law through the body of Christ, that you might belong to another, to Him who was raised from the dead, in order that we might bear fruit for God* (Romans 7:4).

BIBLICAL METAPHORS OF OUR DEATH

In his epistles, Paul uses two spiritual pictures to explain our death in Christ: water baptism and circumcision.

Water Baptism

*...We are those who have **died to sin; how can we live in it any longer?** Or don't you know that all of us who were baptized into Christ Jesus were baptized into His death? **We were** therefore buried with Him through baptism into death in order that, just as Christ was raised from the dead through the glory of the Father, we too may live a new life* (Romans 6:2-4).

Water baptism is an event, not a process. If water baptism took longer than a single dunk, it would be better named *a drowning!*

Circumcision

> *In Him you were also **circumcised** with a **circumcision** not performed by human hands. Your whole self ruled by the flesh was put off when you were **circumcised** by Christ, having been **buried with Him in baptism,** in which you were also raised with Him through your faith in the working of God, who raised Him from the dead.*
>
> *When you were dead in your sins and in the **uncircumcision of your flesh**, God made you alive with Christ. He forgave us all our sins, having canceled the charge of our legal indebtedness, which stood against us and condemned us; He has taken it away, nailing it to the cross* (Colossians 2:11-14).

Thank God that circumcision is a one-time, past-tense event, and not an ongoing process!

Ouch!

These two metaphors show even more clearly how our death was completed in Christ. We do not have to die daily, in the same way that we do not have to be baptized daily or circumcised daily.

What about the Christian cliché, which says, "Death must precede resurrection"? This statement implies that Christians must kill their flesh before they are able to walk in the Spirit and in victory. This is a slight distortion of the truth; the statement is true, but the application is not.

The truth is that nonbelievers live their lives in death; they are separated from God and without hope in this world. According to Ephesians 2:5, *"when we were dead in trespasses, [He] made us alive together with Christ...."* (NKJV). When nonbelievers accept the death and resurrection of the Savior (which includes their being crucified in Him) they step into the newness of life in Christ.

To continue to try to crucify the flesh shows that one does not understand what Christ accomplished.

> *For Christ also suffered once for sins, the righteous for the unrighteous, to bring you to God. He was put to death in the body but made alive in the Spirit* (1 Peter 3:18).

God has already completed this work. It is an insult to try to add to what He has done, as though it were insufficient! There is no place in the Christian life for people to put themselves to death. *Once you are in Christ, you never have to die again.* Jesus put you inside Himself on the cross; the whole rest of the New Testament points back at the fact that your death in Christ is a totally accomplished, one-time, past-tense event—*not* a process or a present work.

Unfortunately, most believers have been taught to fight or crucify the flesh. They see themselves as being caught in a lifelong battle between the two natures resident within them. I call these folks "spiritually suicidal." Instead of simply receiving and dwelling in Christ's victory over the flesh, they spend their whole lives trying to do what Jesus has already done and trying to defeat what He has already defeated for them. What a waste!

Not only has your flesh nature already been completely removed from you, but the writers of the New Testament didn't even expect Christians to sin. For example, the apostle John clearly believed that Christians were free to walk in a completely sinless life:

> *My dear children, **I write this to you so that you will not sin. But if** anybody does sin, we have an advocate with the Father—Jesus Christ, the Righteous One. He is the atoning sacrifice for our sins, and not only for ours but also for the sins of the whole world* (1 John 2:1-2).

I love how the apostle said, *"But if."* John expected them to walk in a sinless life—*"But if"* was merely a backup!

I DIE DAILY

At this point, some might object and remind me that Jesus said to pick up your cross *daily*, as if to refer to a life of self-crucifixion. Only in Luke 9:23 did Jesus say the word *daily* in regard to taking up one's cross. Actually, the word *daily* does not appear in many of the original manuscripts, but even if it is there, it does not change what Jesus was talking about.

Jesus was not suggesting that we have to crucify ourselves every day. He was speaking of the ongoing trial of being His follower. This speaks of rejection and persecution, not a daily battle with the flesh, as many have mistakenly assumed.

Others hold to the idea of a daily self-crucifixion because the apostle Paul said that he "died daily." Personally, I was shocked when I looked in my concordance and found that I had been taught entirely incorrectly regarding this concept. Other than the one mention (which may or may not actually be in Luke 9:23), Paul's famous *dying daily* is used just once—and it is not about dealing with the flesh.

> *And as for us, why do we endanger ourselves every hour?* ***I face death every day*** *["I die daily" in the King James Version]—yes, just as surely as I boast about you in Christ Jesus our Lord. If I fought wild beasts in Ephesus with no more than human hopes, what have I gained? If the dead are not raised, "Let us eat and drink, for tomorrow we die"* (1 Corinthians 15:30-32).

In verse 30 Paul wrote of being in danger every day, and in verse 32 he spoke of fighting wild beasts. Paul was not talking about how he dealt with the flesh; he was describing the persecution that he suffered for following Christ.

In summary, we are not in an ongoing battle with the flesh. It was put to death at the cross of Christ. As long as we think that we must die, crucify ourselves, or fight against our flesh, *we continue believing a lie.* This lie keeps countless people locked in a never-ending battle against their flesh—a battle Jesus has already fought and won.

Now that we know the truth—that our flesh was put to death on the cross—how do we understand the ongoing battle against sin?

STILL STRUGGLING?

At this point, the Christian man who struggles daily with the temptations of lust will say that, even though the death of the flesh is a past-tense event, the battle is present tense. Many find comfort in relating to the words of Paul in Romans chapter 7.

It has been wrongly taught that this passage was written of Paul's struggle against sin while he was a believer. However, when read in context, it becomes obvious that Paul was using a form of speech called the *historical present.*

The main verses that are quoted by the struggling believer are Romans 7:14-25, but we will examine these over the coming pages in the larger context of Romans 7:1–8:4 to get the true tense and, therefore, the true sense of the passage. Let's begin with the first half of chapter 7:

> *Do you not know, brothers and sisters—for I am speaking to those who know the law—that the law has authority over someone only as long as that person lives? For example, by law a married woman is bound to her husband as long as he is alive, but if her husband dies, she is released from the law that binds her to him. So then, if she has sexual relations with another man while her husband is still alive, she is called an adulteress. But if her husband dies, she is released from that law and is not an adulteress if she marries another man.*

*So, my brothers and sisters, **you also died** to the law through the body of Christ that you might belong to another, to Him who was raised from the dead, in order that we might bear fruit for God. For **when we were** in the realm of the flesh, the sinful passions aroused by the law **were at work** in us, so that we bore fruit for death. But now, by dying to what once bound us, **we have been released** from the law so that we serve in the new way of the Spirit, and not in the old way of the written code.*

*What shall we say, then? Is the law sinful? Certainly not! Nevertheless, **I would not have known** what sin was had it not been for the law. For **I would not have known** what coveting really was if the law had not said, "You shall not covet." But sin, seizing the opportunity afforded by the commandment, produced in me every kind of coveting. For apart from the law, sin was dead. **Once I was alive** apart from the law; but when the commandment came, sin sprang to life and **I died**. I found that the very commandment that was intended to bring life actually brought death. For sin, seizing the opportunity afforded by the commandment, deceived me, and through the commandment **put me to death**. So then, the law is holy, and the commandment is holy, righteous and good* (Romans 7:1-12).

So far, Romans speaks of what Paul found to be the truth, in the *past tense*. Every underlined statement shows that He has already found his complete freedom from law and sin, *past tense*.

To understand Romans 7:14-25, we must understand the *historical present* voice, which employs the present tense in narrating past events. Literary critics and grammarians claim that the historical present has the effect of making past events more vivid.

Notice how the verbs in the following excerpt from Charles Dickens' novel, *David Copperfield*, shift from the past tense to the historical present, giving the reader the sense of being there as the story unfolds.

> If the funeral had been yesterday, I could not recollect it better. The very air of the best parlour, when I went in at the door, the bright condition of the fire, the shining of the wine in the decanters, the patterns of the glasses and plates, the faint sweet smell of cake, the odour of Miss Murdstone's dress, and our black clothes. Mr Chillip is [past tense: would be was] in the room, and comes [past tense: came] to speak to me.
>
> 'And how is Master David?' he says [past tense: said] kindly.
>
> I cannot [past tense: could not] tell him very well. I give [past tense: gave] him my hand, which he holds [past tense: held] in his.[1]

Here is a more personal example of switching from the past tense to the historical present.

> I remember summer camp like it was yesterday. I remember sitting around the campfire with my friends, making s'mores, laughing, and singing songs. Tim is shouting about something, but I am not paying any attention. Instead, I am entranced by the flickering flames. The smoke engulfs me and I know that tomorrow the scent in my sweater will be a constant reminder of tonight's fun.

See how subtle the change is from speaking past tense to speaking in the historical present? In Romans, Paul subtly switches from speaking in the past tense (see Rom. 7:1-12) to speaking in the historical present (see Rom. 7:14-25). In the latter section, he writes in the voice of the nonbeliever who is trying to live right and be a good person, apart from the power of being in Christ.[2]

Many modern Christians have been *misled;* as a result, they believe Paul's words indicate that believers will continue to struggle with sin. Yet, Paul had already laid the premise for this section—he was completely free.

> *Did that which is good, then, become death to me? By no means! Nevertheless, in order that sin might be recognized as sin, it used what is good to bring about my death, so that through the commandment sin might become utterly sinful.*
>
> *We know that the law is spiritual; but I am unspiritual, sold as a slave to sin. I do not understand what I do. For what I want to do I do not do, but what I hate I do. And if I do what I do not want to do, I agree that the law is good. As it is, it is no longer I myself who do it, but it is sin living in me. For I know that good itself does not dwell in me, that is, in my sinful nature. For I have the desire to do what is good, but I cannot carry it out. For I do not do the good I want to do, but the evil I do not want to do—this I keep on doing. Now if I do what I do not want to do, it is no longer I who do it, but it is sin living in me that does it.*
>
> *So I find this law at work: Although I want to do good, evil is right there with me. For in my inner being I delight in God's law; but I see another law at work in me, waging war against the law of my mind and making me a prisoner of the law of sin at work within me. What a wretched man I am! Who will rescue me from this body that is subject to death?* (Romans 7:13-24)

It becomes glaringly obvious that Paul was not writing of his current/present struggles when we see the context. He lays the premise—he is completely free. Then Paul describes in the historical present tense what his life felt like as a Pharisee trying to live right before he received Jesus or had the indwelling Holy Spirit. Paul then picks up with the good news again—he was set free by what Christ did on the cross!

> *Thanks be to God, who delivers me through Jesus Christ our Lord!*
>
> *So then, I myself in my mind am a slave to God's law, but in my sinful nature a slave to the law of sin.*
>
> *Therefore, there is now no condemnation for those who are in Christ Jesus,* **because through Christ Jesus** *the law of the Spirit who gives life* **has set you free** *from the law of sin and death. For what the law was powerless to do because it was weakened by the flesh,* **God did** *by sending His own Son in the likeness of sinful flesh to be a sin offering. And so He condemned sin in the flesh, in order that the righteous requirement of the law might be fully met in us, who do not live according to the flesh but according to the Spirit* (Romans 7:25–8:4).

Even though many Christians have found comfort in relating to Romans 7, Paul was not writing of his Christian life. By reading this incorrectly, many have *found an excuse for ongoing fleshly behavior.* How grieving this interpretation is to the Holy Spirit! (At the end of this section, you'll find a more in-depth explanation of two common objections to my views of Romans 7.)

Though we might struggle in removing sin from our daily lives, we can find no camaraderie or solace in the idea of Paul struggling with the flesh after salvation. So with the Romans chapter 7 myth dismantled, the question remains: *How do we understand our current ongoing struggle against sin?*

Although the crucifixion of the flesh is a past-tense, fully accomplished event, there are two words that explain our current situation. The New Testament uses the words *put* and *rid* regarding our ongoing struggle against sin.

The classic novel *The Strange Case of Dr. Jekyll and Mr. Hyde*, by Robert Louis Stevenson, is a great picture of how the unbeliever in Romans 7:14-24 struggles between being good and evil. Stevenson wrote of the gracious Dr. Jekyll who had created a potion that divided his good nature from his evil one. The dark nature took form in the character of the disfigured Mr. Hyde, who went about doing evil. This tale from 1886 is a stunning picture of how non-Christians helplessly struggle against their evil nature. But no Christian should ever be able to relate to Dr. Jekyll and Mr. Hyde, because our Mr. Hyde (the flesh) was crucified with Christ, and our Dr. Jekyll (the good nature) is empowered by God's grace.

Even though Mr. Hyde has been removed from us, and we now live only as Dr. Jekyll, there still remains a process of *putting off* and *ridding ourselves* of the clothes that we wore as Mr. Hyde.

Unfortunately, many Christians see Mr. Hyde's clothes in the closet and assume that he must be alive in the house somewhere. Many Christians run around looking for Mr. Hyde so that they can "crucify" him daily. They are looking for someone who is no longer there! Instead, we must stop wearing his old clothes. Mr. Hyde (the flesh) is gone. Nevertheless, he lived in the same "house" with us for many years and everything that belonged to him must be thrown out!

Just because an individual continues to choose to sin does not mean that the flesh is alive. Jesus caused a complete death and there is nothing we can do to resurrect the flesh. There is not one verse in the New Testament that refers to a Christian having the ability to raise his or her flesh from the dead.[3]

In the Garden of Eden, Adam and Eve were able to choose to sin, *even though they didn't have a sin nature*. This is the perfect picture of the Christian. Jesus has removed our sin nature from us, yet at times we still choose to commit sins. Every day, we get to choose whether or not to eat the forbidden fruit. Even if we choose to eat it, it is not the old (dead) sin nature driving us to do it. Our failure does not mean that our flesh has returned. Yes, the demonic suggestion tries to convince us of what is false: that if we sin, then our flesh is alive. But it is simply not true.

The ongoing removal of sinful actions from our life is a process of choosing to stop doing what used to be natural for us when we lived out of the flesh nature. Sin is no longer natural for us because, with the sin nature removed, we must literally fight our own divine nature in order to choose sin. That is why we feel conviction, because sinful actions run against the grain of our new nature and identity.

We need a correct perspective toward the flesh: it is a completely defeated foe and its remnants have nothing in common with our identity. We must make the choice to no longer choose sinful actions. But be encouraged—this is progressive and gets easier over time.

Objections and Answers to Romans 7 as a Description of Paul's Pre-Conversion State

The following are the objections I mentioned earlier; they will help you field your own questions and the questions of others.

Objection 1: In Romans 6, Paul lays out the basis of a life with victory over sin; yet in chapter 7 he seems to relate to the common experience of so many Christians, followed by the more mature walk in the Spirit described in chapter 8. Isn't it right to read the flow of these three chapters as progressive?

Answer: Actually in Romans chapter 6 and 7 there is not a building flow as many have taught. These two chapters are structured around four separate questions that are being asked and answered. Here are the four questions:

1. *"What shall we say then? Shall we go on sinning so that grace may increase? By no means!"* (Romans 6:1-2a).

2. *"What then? Shall we sin because we are not under the law but under grace? By no means!"* (Romans 6:15).

3. *"What shall we say then? Is the law sinful? Certainly not!"* (Romans 7:7a).

4. *"Did that which is good then become death to me? By no means!"* (Romans 7:13a).

Romans 7:14-25 is not built upon Romans 6; in fact, it is answering a completely different question. It is important that we take Paul's writing in 7:14-25 as a response to the question posed in 7:13; that is the accurate context. Romans 6 and 7 should not be read as a progressive flow, but as Paul asking and answering four different questions.

Objection 2: To say that Paul was struggling against sin before he was a Christian doesn't make sense to me because I don't understand why a sinner would be struggling against sin?

Answer: Many Christians seem to think that non-Christians don't struggle between choosing right and wrong, as if they are conscienceless beings. This is simply not true. A great picture of the Romans 7, pre-conversion man is found in the true meaning of the word *jihad*:

Jihad: A striving for perfection, frequently used within Islam. Usually, the term refers to an internal struggle that a person has with their imperfections. The term is also used to refer to a defensive war. Some radical Fundamentalist Muslims and the Western media often interpret the term as a synonym for an aggressive "holy war."[4]

The typical Muslim sees the "holy war" of jihad to be an inner struggle against sin. Also the term *infidel,* would be similar to the Christian understanding of "the flesh." So for a Muslim to say, "I am in a holy war against the infidel" would be synonymous with a Christian saying, "I am in a war trying to kill my flesh nature." With this understanding we are able to see that there are over a billion non-Christians trapped in a Romans 7 type of struggle. It is very common for the non-Christian who is bound in a false religion to feel the powerless struggle of the Romans 7 man.

PUTTING OFF THE FLESH

Put is an amazing word. In the New Testament there are 29 different Greek root words used for the word *put.* In the following verses we can see how the Bible directs us to *put off* and *rid ourselves* of the garments (the old clothes) of our flesh (since the flesh is dead and buried in Christ, the flesh no longer needs any clothes). This is *not* something *to work at* doing. Instead, think of putting off as simply *acknowledging* that the flesh is dead, and therefore we no longer need to live as though it were still alive!

"Put" and "Put Off" (As in Removing a Garment)

> *In Him you were also circumcised with a circumcision not performed by human hands. Your whole self ruled by the flesh was **put off** when **you were** circumcised by Christ...* (Colossians 2:11).

Notice in the above verse that our flesh nature *was* put off—past tense.

> *For if you live according to the flesh, you will die; but if by the Spirit you **put** to death the misdeeds of the body, you will live* (Romans 8:13).

In this verse, we are not putting to death our "flesh nature"; we are putting off "deeds."

> *When I was a child, I talked like a child, I thought like a child, I reasoned like a child. When I became a man, I **put** the ways of childhood behind me* (1 Corinthians 13:11).

(Many times the word *put* is used similarly to the word *placed*.)

> *But as for you, not in this manner did you learn the Christ, since, indeed, as is the case, you heard and in Him were taught just as truth is in Jesus, that **you have put off once for all** with reference to your former manner of life the old self who is being corrupted according to the passionate desires of deceit; moreover, that you are being constantly renewed with reference to the spirit of your mind; and that **you have put on once for all** the new self who after God was created in righteousness and holiness of truth* (Ephesians 4:20-24 Wuest).

> *Therefore each of you must **put off** falsehood and speak truthfully to your neighbor, for we are all members of one body* (Ephesians 4:25).

Paul says to "put off" lying, which means to remove it from our lives.

> ***Put** to death, therefore, whatever belongs to your earthly nature: sexual immorality, impurity, lust, evil desires and greed, which is idolatry* (Colossians 3:5).

The above verse is not calling us to be executioners. It is talking about placing our earthly nature in the grave. In other words, "Don't carry that dead thing around!"

"Rid"

*Get **rid** of all bitterness, rage and anger, brawling and slander, along with every form of malice* (Ephesians 4:31).

*But now you must also **rid** yourselves of all such things as these: anger, rage, malice, slander, and filthy language from your lips* (Colossians 3:8).

*Therefore, get **rid** of all moral filth and the evil that is so prevalent and humbly accept the word planted in you, which can save you* (James 1:21).

*Therefore, **rid** yourselves of all malice and all deceit, hypocrisy, envy, and slander of every kind* (1 Peter 2:1).

PUTTING ON THE NEW MAN

Not only does the Word direct us to put off certain things, but there are also many things that Scripture tells us to *put on*. Many Christians have taken the phrase *put on* and have tried to use it as a formula. For example, there are those who daily declare, "I choose today to *put on* the armor of God." They also work and work, trying to *put on* the new man; but this was not the intention of the New Testament writers' instructions to *put on* the new man.

The New Testament phrase translated "put on" comes from the Greek root word *enduo*, which means "to sink into."[5] *Putting on* Christ does not mean that we must work and strive in human efforts to be like Christ. *Putting on* Christ means to sink into Christ, to lean back and rest in our identity in Christ. Keep this in mind as you read the following verses. By sinking into Christ we can, as Paul wrote, *"...live up to what we have already attained"* (Phil. 3:16).

"Put On" (As in Sink Into)

> *The night is nearly over; the day is almost here. So let us put aside the deeds of darkness and **put on** the armor of light* (Romans 13:12).

> *And to **put on** the new self, created to be like God in true righteousness and holiness* (Ephesians 4:24).

> ***Put on** the full armor of God, so that you can take your stand against the devil's schemes* (Ephesians 6:11).

> *Therefore **put on** the full armor of God, so that when the day of evil comes, you may be able to stand your ground, and after you have done everything, to stand* (Ephesians 6:13).

> *Whatever you have learned or received or heard from me, or seen in me—**put** it into practice. And the God of peace will be with you* (Philippians 4:9).

> *And have **put on** the new self, which is being renewed in knowledge in the image of its Creator* (Colossians 3:10).

> *But since we belong to the day, let us be sober, **putting on** faith and love as a breastplate, and the hope of salvation as a helmet* (1 Thessalonians 5:8).

> *And over all these virtues **put on** love, which binds them all together in perfect unity* (Colossians 3:14).

Through these verses we can see that the "putting on" that Paul talks about in his epistles is not based in human striving, but in a *sinking into* the provision of grace and new life through Christ's death on the cross. This is incredible news for many believers, who, because of wrong teaching, have been working hard to die to themselves and crucify their flesh daily. How freeing it is to simply receive Christ's accomplished work on our behalf and to believe in our *new* nature—which is inclined to do good, not evil.

This revelation is monumental in getting breakthrough in sexual temptation. Once you realize that your struggle against your flesh and sin nature is actually a myth, you will be empowered to put off the leftover "clothing" of your old nature and begin living according to the righteousness of Christ, which is your new nature.

Tool

Consider the sin issues that keep rearing their heads in your life: lust, anger, greed, arrogance, etc. Now close your eyes and relax.

Imagine yourself inside a house. First recognize that Mr. Hyde (your sin nature) has been crucified; therefore he no longer resides in the house. However, his belongings are still present. Notice in the closet the clothes he used to wear: the jacket of lust, the belt of greed, the shoes of arrogance, the walking cane of anger.

Stop in front of the closet and pause. First, thank Jesus for having removed the flesh and sin nature from you at the cross. Then ask Him to help you carry Hyde's old clothes out to the yard. Once you and Jesus take the clothes outside, imagine yourself pouring several gallons of gasoline on the pile and flicking a match atop that junk.

Feel free to watch it burn. This simple exercise is one way to acknowledge the fact that your old nature was put off, but there is a process of putting off the deeds of the old nature.

Next we must "put on," and this is even simpler. Simply close your eyes again, only this time have your arms outstretched at your sides, opened wide. Imagine the Lord placing a robe over you, on which the following words are written: "His Righteousness." Feel yourself sink into it and its marvelous freedom. Remind yourself often that you have *put off* and now you must simply *sink into* everything you have been given in Christ.

CHAPTER 6

YOU ARE A
NEW CREATION

*Therefore, if anyone is in Christ, he is a
new creation; old things have passed away;
behold, all things have become new.*
—2 CORINTHIANS 5:17 NKJV

Sitting in a Denny's restaurant at 2 A.M. talking about masturbation is not what I consider "a good time." Yet there I was across the table from my friend Larry, who had called to see if I was available to talk.

Drearily the waitress asked, "Would you like more coffee?"

I responded, "Yes, please," fully aware that I had a long night ahead.

Larry began, "Well as I said before, I just can't seem to stop looking at porn. I don't know man, am I an addict?"

"Whoa!" I said, "Before you go labeling yourself and messing with your identity, how about we back up a little."

He started again, "I just can't stop watching the free porn on the Internet. Being a single guy I have a thousand justifications: I am not hurting anyone, it is hidden, everyone is doing it, and last but not least—why not?"

"OK bud, that is a list I totally understand. Your last reason actually is the most important one to look at: 'Why *not*?' This is the million-dollar question of the night. Why not look at porn?"

I said this just as our waitress delivered our food. Having overheard my last statement, she was a little awkward, but hey, I should have been at home snuggled comfortably in my bed anyway; I was bound to say *something* embarrassing!

"Why not look at porn..." He seemed to be mulling the question over under his breath.

"Larry, if you can understand the answer to that question, then the issue will be completely solved." He looked at me incredulously, as if I were baiting him into a philosophical pursuit.

"No Larry, I am serious. The answer to that question is the answer to your issue! I am not messing with you. If you grasp the answer to that question, then that is the truth that will set you free."

"OK, Jonathan," he said with a slow thoughtfulness. "I guess the main reasons I have heard for why I shouldn't look at porn are: it is a sin, it distorts my view of intimacy, it demeans and objectifies women, and it is addictive."

"That is a pretty standard list of reasons why you shouldn't look at porn," I said in agreement. "But none of those are the answer that you need to grasp to be free."

"OK, smarty-pants" he said humorously, "What *is* the right answer to the question?"

"OK, remember how I have shared with you in previous conversations that every man struggling with temptation needs to realize that his flesh nature has been crucified, satan is a defeated foe, and the law is powerless to help him? In addition to that, I have talked about how we need to view women as sisters and not objects of selfish pleasure, and how a person's identity does not come from his actions, but from the identity God has given him."

Larry was all ears at this point.

"Yet understanding these truths alone is not enough to bring full and lasting freedom. There is one more major key which must be grasped to answer the question, 'Why shouldn't I look at porn?' To understand this key, let me illustrate from the story of Nehemiah. Do you have a Bible on your smartphone?"

"Yes," he said.

"OK. Look up Nehemiah 6:11."

"But I said [Nehemiah narrating], *'Should a man like me run away? Or should one like me go into the temple to save his life? I will not go!'"*

"Larry, in this story Nehemiah's enemies were trying to use fear tactics to intimidate him to step into sin. The reason that Nehemiah didn't fall into their trap was because he knew who he was. If only men knew who they were in Christ they would be able to say, "Should a man like me look at pornography? I will not!"

"Whoa...that is amazing. So you are saying that if I understood my identity and walked in it, it would answer the question of why I don't look at porn?"

"Let me ask you this: As a new creation, have you ever thought about what Christ made you into?" I asked. (See Second Corinthians 5:17.)

"How do you figure?"

"Well," I continued, "if we have been made into something new, then what have we been made into? Do you have a new nature? How different are you from what you were?"

"I guess I never really thought what it means to be a new creation..." Larry said thoughtfully.

"Larry, do you realize that at this very moment you are completely righteous?" (See Romans 5:17; First Corinthians 1:30; Romans 6:17-18;

Second Corinthians 5:21; Hebrews 10:14; Ephesians 4:24; First Peter 1:13-16; First Corinthians 6:11.)

"Ha! You are, kidding right?" he said, a little stunned. I guess he wasn't expecting to hear that from me when we sat down at 2 A.M. to talk about his porn-viewing.

"I am not kidding. The Bible is very clear that Christ has already accomplished the work of making you righteous."

"But my pastor regularly tells me that my heart is desperately wicked, so how can I be righteous?" (See Jeremiah 17:9.)

"Actually, Larry, that verse is more accurately translated as 'the heart is beyond cure.' That is why Jesus came and gave us a new heart, because the old one was incurable. As a new creation, you have a spiritually God-given new heart!" (See Ezekiel 36:25-27; 11:19-20; Jeremiah 31:33-34; Hebrews 8:10.)

"Come on man, do you honestly believe that I have a new heart and I am righteous? What about in Isaiah where it says that God's ways are not my ways and God's thoughts are not my thoughts? I regularly feel like I can relate to that verse!" he said. (See Isaiah 55:8.)

"That verse was true of us," I said. "But again, we have been made into new creations, and God has not only given us a new heart, but also a new mind. We have been given the mind of Christ. With the mind of Christ, it is no longer true to say of us that our thoughts are not His thoughts and His ways are not our ways." (See Romans 12:2; First Corinthians 2:16.)

"Oh man, this is too much!" he said with a bewildered look. "Are you saying that I have believed wrong things about my identity which actually drag me down and actually keep me from living as a new creation?"

"That is exactly what I am saying!"

"OK Jon, what about my righteousness being as filthy rags? That's another verse I have clung to for years." (See Isaiah 64:6.)

"Your righteousness *was* as filthy rags; that is why the Bible says Christ has become your righteousness!" (See First Corinthians 1:30; Second Corinthians 5:21; Romans 5:17.)

"So...what you are saying...is that I wasn't righteous; I didn't think like God, and I didn't have His heart, but then Jesus came and reversed all of that? Yet, I am continuing to live like the old creation because I don't understand or believe that I am a new creation?" Larry seemed noticeably strained, but he was starting to grasp what I was saying.

"Let me ask you a few questions," I said. "What is your nature?"

"Huh? What do you mean?" he replied.

"If when you were born, you inherited the nature of Adam, the so-called sin nature, then it would stand to reason that Christ didn't just give you a new heart and mind, but also a new nature, right?"

"Yeah, I am following you," he said.

"So can a father produce a son of a different nature? By that I mean, humans produce humans; cats produce cats; cows produce cows; and divinity produces—" Larry looked at me in astonishment.

"Jonathan, you can't mean—that just sounds too far-fetched. If you said that publicly, people would stone you on the Internet!" remarked a very concerned Larry.

"Seriously. Consider again the truth that we are called the children of God and that we are made in His image and likeness. Don't all children carry the very same DNA as their parents? I believe that is why the apostle Peter wrote that we are partakers of God's divine nature. God has given us a new nature; actually, He has given us *His* nature!" (See John 3:8; Second Peter 1:4; Hebrews 3:14; First John 3:1-2.)

"Shall I go on?"

"Yes, I need to hear this!" he said eagerly. He was becoming more alert and interested at this point. I glanced at my cell phone; it read 2:35 A.M. *No problem. I am a night owl anyway,* or so I reasoned, as I took a long sip of coffee.

"OK Larry, let me ask you another question. Are you worthy of the death of Jesus on the cross?"

He gave a long pause while chewing his oversized burger. "I don't think so. I guess I have heard all my life how I am totally depraved, evil, and sinful. So how could I be worth the death of Jesus?"

"Larry, do you believe that God is dumb?"

"No," said a surprised Larry.

"Are you sure that God isn't stupid?" I pushed harder.

"Nope," he said defensively.

"Actually, Larry, I agree with you. God isn't dumb, nor is He stupid. In fact, I believe that God is the most brilliant thinker and makes the most intelligent investments that could possibly be made."

"Yeah, so?" said Larry, trying to see where I was going with this line of reasoning.

"So if God is a good investor, He did not take the most valuable thing in Heaven—Jesus—and trade Him for what the Father would consider a piece of trash. Apparently God perceived that you were worth the death of Jesus. The Father didn't get a raw deal. Maybe you have underestimated your value and worth?"

I continued, "Value is determined by what a person is willing to pay for something. If God was willing to purchase you by the death of Jesus, then apparently your value is equivalent to that of Jesus. You are worth the blood of Jesus, and according to the Father, you are a good investment!"

"Whoa, I have never thought about it like that before!" he replied, noticeably excited.

"Yeah, most people have not truly seen their value through God's point of view. Once we can view ourselves His way, our lives will agree with what He says about us. Are you ready to hear some even heavier truth?"

"Give me both barrels!" he said with anticipation.

"Here goes. Remember how the apostle Paul rebuked the Corinthians for thinking like mere humans? Can you imagine being rebuked for thinking like a human? Paul expected that they shouldn't live on such a low level! Paul taught that we are filled with all of God. We have not just been given the Holy Spirit; we have actually been made one with the Spirit of God! In the same way that Jesus was full of God, so are we!" (See First Corinthians 3:1-3; Ephesians 3:19; Colossians 1:19; 2:9-10; First Corinthians 6:17.)

I continued unloading both "barrels" of truth. "The apostle John taught that we are designed to live just like Jesus! And he said that *'as He* [Jesus] *is, so are we in this world.'* This is not in reference to the Jesus of the past—the Suffering Servant; this is in reference to the present-tense Jesus—the reigning, righteous King, full of grace. These are the attributes that now describe us, *'...who receive God's abundant provision of grace and of the gift of righteousness reign in life through the one man, Jesus Christ...'* 'As He is, so are we.' Or to paraphrase, if it is true of Jesus, it should be true of us!" (See First John 2:6; 3:2; 4:17 NKJV; Romans 5:17.)

"Jon, that is a lot to take in. I feel like the room is spinning!"

"I know man; that is a bit much for 2:54 in the morning, huh?"

"It is very stretching, because I have never heard this perspective before...but it is biblically sound."

I said, "Before we go get some sleep, allow me to summarize. Proverbs 23:7 says, *'As* [a man] *thinks in his heart, so is he'* (NKJV).

So if you were taught to see yourself as a mere human, one who does not think like God, with a desperately wicked heart and even your righteousness is as a filthy rag, then you would live life under that perspective.

"In contrast, the Bible teaches that God gave you a new heart, mind, and spirit...that you are one spirit with God and filled with His fullness. You are the righteousness of God in Christ, you are a partaker of the divine nature, and as He is, so are you in this world! If you would come into agreement with the Word and believe what God says about you, then your life would come into agreement.

"As Paul wrote, *'Only let us live up to what we have already attained.'* The problem for most Christians is that they have never been taught these things, and those who have, typically don't believe it." (See Philippians 3:16.)

Larry said with a slowness that was palpable, "You are saying that the answer to 'Why not look at porn?' is that my identity has changed and now I am completely incompatible with pornography! And I can say similarly with Nehemiah, 'Should a man like me look at pornography? I will not!' WOW, it may take me awhile, but I want to renew my mind to the truths you have dropped on me tonight."

"I understand; it took a season of meditating on these truths before I could fully grasp them myself.[1] And for the future, maybe we should eat at IHOP; my appetizer sampler is like lead in my belly."

"Ha-ha, no problem, bro!"

Tool

Copy and post this prayer in several places so that you can pray through it regularly:

> *Lord, thank You that I am a new creation. You have made me holy, righteous, and perfect. You have completely sanctified me and made me in Your image and Your likeness. You have conformed me into the image of Your Son. You have filled me with the fullness of the Godhead.*
>
> *I ask that You would burn these truths into my heart and renew my mind with them until I am completely transformed. Thank You for crucifying and putting off my old nature; I choose this day to sink into Christ. I am a partaker*

of Your divine nature; I am a receiver of Your abundant grace and Your gift of righteousness.

I will not look over my shoulder at the past; I will not follow the voice of a stranger. Instead, I focus on being seated with You in the heavenly places. You have given me Your mind, Your Spirit, and Your heart. You have made me Your ambassador. I am now one spirit with You. Therefore, I choose to live this day just as Jesus would in this Earth. I will think like Him, walk like Him, and love like Him. Because, as He is, so am I in this Earth!

SECTION 1 SUMMARY

It is essential for a Christian man to understand that he is powerful and that he is the only one in charge of his emotions, responses, and decisions. He does not get to choose what life hands him, but he always gets to choose what he will do in response. There are only two options in life—make a powerful decision to walk in love, or make a powerless choice to walk otherwise.

Your identity is not the sum of your actions. Your identity flows from who God says that you are. You must understand who God says you are and come into agreement with Him; then your actions will change.

The "spiritually suicidal" branch of Christianity—that is, those who are still trying to kill their flesh—will never see success. We must lay aside this terrible doctrine once and for all. It is time to sink into Christ and rest in the work He has already accomplished on our behalf.

It is time to grasp the revelation of who we are as new creations in Christ. We cannot afford to continue wallowing in our past condition as totally depraved, filthy rags, and so forth. We must realize that what God says about us is truer than what we think of ourselves.

SECTION 2

Who Is the Enemy?

Many have been taught that the devil is like a puppet master pulling all the strings of temptation behind the scenes. That old, crafty tempter is working overtime to get Christians addicted to their lusts. We will look in this section at the current work of the devil and how to stand against him.

Christians like rules, especially when they might feel safer or more righteous by setting these rules. Yet those who try to use the law to insulate themselves from sin actually empower sin! So what is a Christian man to do?

A common teaching regarding temptation is this: If temptation can be avoided, then sin can be avoided. This idea implies that people should do all they can to remove temptation from their lives. Yet, when God created the Garden of Eden, He placed the forbidden tree in the middle of The Garden. With this in mind, how should a Christian understand and interact with temptation?

This question is important, because the weight of shame has crushed many good Christians. Guilt, shame, and condemnation keep believers from stepping into their true identity in Christ and from walking with a clean conscience.

Finally, we can rest assured that none of us will live perfect lives. It is important, therefore, to know how to get back up when we fall.

CHAPTER 7

THE DEVIL

The devil made me do it!
—FLIP WILSON

When a Christian man struggles against lust on a regular basis, it is natural for him to begin to view his habit as the product of demonic forces at work in his life. The reality is that, most often, demonic forces are at work, but not in the ways that we might think. Most true spiritual warfare takes place in the arena of *truth versus lies.* The devil is a liar, and he uses his craftiness to get us to lay aside our identity and authority. Our battle must be understood as a battle to maintain our identity, because the authority we have been given as believers is contained in our identity.

Many Christian men have reached a point emotionally where they feel as though they have been stripped of their armor. They are being beaten to a pulp. They have been chained and are being dragged behind the devil's chariot as his spoils of war. Churches are filled with Christian men who feel in their hearts like Samson in the bottom of the prison. It is time that we understand what the Bible says about our identity so that we can get our authority back!

The truth regarding our identity is that we have been put into Christ. *"For in Him we live and move and have our being"* (Acts 17:28). We abide in Him, and He in us (see John 15:4). We have been seated with Him in heavenly places (see Eph. 2:6). *"Greater is He who is in* [us] *than he who is in the world"* (1 John 4:4 NASB).

We should experience the truth of being *"more than conquerors"* (Rom. 8:37). Christians should be able to truly declare: *"I can do all this through Him who gives me strength"* (Phil. 4:13). The Word tells us that we are one in spirit with Him (see 1 Cor. 6:17). Therefore, the authority that we see in the life of Jesus is the authority that we have been given. He gave us the keys of the Kingdom of Heaven (see Matt. 16:19).

With powerful Scriptures like these, how is it that Christian men continue to struggle to have authority in this arena? It is because when men lose their hold on their identities, they lose their grip on their authority. There is no question about us having all authority so long as we comprehend our true identity in Christ. If we understand that we abide in Him (which also means that we abide in His authority), then our spiritual warfare is very different: we are not fighting *for* victory; we are fighting *from* victory.

Many men continue fighting and fighting, but it is time to realize that Jesus already won the battle—and then He put us inside of Him to share this victory! Every Christian is inside of Christ, regardless of whether they are behaving perfectly or not.

> *And this is the testimony: God has given us eternal life, and this life is **in His Son.** Whoever has the Son has life; whoever does not have the Son of God does not have life* (1 John 5:11-12).

With the foundation that we are in Christ and share in His authority over the devil, let's dive deeper into examining how utterly defeated the devil truly is.

The apostle Paul wrote much on the subject of spiritual warfare in the New Testament. Yet because of cultural differences, we have overlooked some of his best insights.

For example, we miss a lot of the meaning in Colossians 2:15, which says, *"And having disarmed the powers and authorities, He made a public spectacle of them, triumphing over them by the cross."* When Paul uses the word *disarmed* in this passage, he is making a first-century cultural metaphor. Paul is saying that Jesus totally stripped satan of all his power and authority. It was a term used for the disarming of a defeated foe.

The word *triumphing* is another cultural reference. When a Roman general had a notable victory, he was allowed to march his victorious armies through the streets of Rome. Behind his chariot were chained all the kings and leaders he had vanquished. They were stripped naked, chained, and pulled behind the conquering general through the streets. They were publically humiliated and openly branded as his spoils.

Paul speaks of Jesus as a conquering General enjoying a cosmic triumph (see John 12:31). In Jesus' triumphal procession are the powers of evil, beaten forever, for everyone to see. And because we have been put in Him, we are also in the chariot with Jesus.

Satan is now naked and powerless!

While many Christian men feel like they are defeated warriors being dragged behind the devil's chariot, the truth is that the devil is being dragged behind their chariots! It is time for us to realize that we can maintain constant authority over the devil by remembering that we are in the chariot with Jesus! We have triumphed over satan!

We must learn to *maintain* our triumph over the devil. The Lord provided us, not only with total victory, but also with complete triumph. It is important to grasp the difference between these two words: *victory* and *triumph*. For example, at a soccer game, when the end of the game comes, the team with the most goals wins and achieves *victory*.

Triumph is what takes place after victory has been achieved. Triumph is the celebration in the streets, the pubs, and the workplace. Triumph is the jumping up and down, the yelling, and the obnoxious, grandiose boasting that occurs in the face of the losing opponent.

We are not still fighting a battle against satan and we are not looking for victory. We are enforcing and reveling in the victory that is already ours; we are triumphing in our King Jesus. He *"...always leads us in triumph in Christ..."* (2 Cor. 2:14 NKJV).

The devil wants the Church to think that we are fighting him, because he does not want the Church to understand that he has been defeated. Since his defeat was already accomplished, the Church is not on the Earth to try to win a victory. Our starting point is victory, and from there we move forward. We are currently on Earth as ambassadors (see 2 Cor. 5:20; Eph. 6:19-20), enforcing and advancing the application of Jesus' victory.

> *Therefore, since the children share in flesh and blood, He Himself likewise also partook of the same, that through death* ***He might render powerless him who had the power of death, that is, the devil,*** *and might free those who through fear of death were subject to slavery all their lives* (Hebrews 2:14-15 NASB).

This verse is absolutely stunning, and yet it is rarely quoted in the modern spiritual warfare circles. The devil has been rendered powerless by the cross of Christ. That is an amazing truth, worthy of meditation.

Another one of my favorite verses to remember about our enemy, the devil, is found in the Book of Isaiah:

> *Those who see you stare at you, they ponder your fate: "Is this the man who shook the earth and made kingdoms tremble, the man who made the world a wilderness, who overthrew its cities and would not let his captives go home?"* (Isaiah 14:16-17)

There will be a day when the Church looks upon satan and is shocked to see what a pitiful loser he really is. Keeping in mind that he is a total liar who accuses and deceives, what would you like to bet that he has probably talked himself up quite a bit?

If we believe what God says about us and do not buy into the lies of the devil, then we are untouchable by him.

His Only Weapon

Remembering that we are in the chariot with Jesus and our defeated foe, satan, is being dragged behind us, we can see that the ongoing battle of spiritual warfare is simply a matter of resisting our enemy's voice. Even as he is dragged, defeated and pathetic, behind the chariot, he continues to taunt with lies, manipulations, temptation, and accusation, as well as intimidation. These are the only weapons he still has.

According to Scripture, lies are satan's stock and trade:

> *Why is My language not clear to you? Because you are unable to hear what I say. You belong to your father, the devil, and you want to carry out your father's desires. He was a murderer from the beginning, not holding to the truth, for **there is no truth in him. When he lies, he speaks his native language, for he is a liar and the father of lies** (John 8:43-44).*

If we allow ourselves to listen to his voice and then come into any form of agreement with him, we are essentially stepping out of Jesus' chariot, stripping off our royal robes, and chaining ourselves beside satan.

This is the position of defeat to which many Christians have unnecessarily submitted themselves. The battle with the devil is a mind game in which he speaks to us and tries to lure us into agreement with him. One of the main mind games the devil uses is to plant thoughts or temptations in our minds. Then he tells us that these ideas are coming from the evil inside of us. This in turn causes us to condemn ourselves.

Many times I have asked men struggling with all their might against lust if they want to think lustful thoughts; invariably the answer is *no*. Yet the thoughts continue to come. I would suggest that those thoughts are sourced in the voice of a demon that sounds like the old flesh nature the man used to walk in.

This explanation is likely true for many men. That is why we must capture these thoughts and be aware of where they are coming from.

> *For though we live in the world, we do not wage war as the world does. The weapons we fight with are not the weapons of the world. On the contrary, they have divine power to demolish strongholds. We demolish arguments and every pretension that sets itself up against the knowledge of God, and **we take captive every thought** to make it obedient to Christ. And we will be ready to punish every act of disobedience, once your obedience is complete* (2 Corinthians 10:3-6).

We must be on guard against satan's lies. The apostle Paul said that the devil and his schemes should not outwit us, because *"...we are not unaware of his schemes"* (2 Cor. 2:11). Paul also told Timothy that demons have a theology that we Christians must be aware of. These doctrines of demons are subtle and convincing enough to lure Christians away from the faith. Paul wrote: *"The Spirit clearly says that in later times some will abandon the faith and follow deceiving spirits and things taught by demons"* (1 Tim. 4:1). Other translations use the term *doctrines of demons*.

While it is true that the devil goes about like a roaring lion, he is only able to devour those who buy into his lies. If we are aware of his schemes and do not allow him to outwit us, then we never have to end up in the lion's mouth.

> *Be alert and of sober mind. Your enemy the devil prowls around like a roaring lion looking for someone to devour. Resist him, standing firm in the faith...* (1 Peter 5:8-9).

According to the apostle John, we are literally untouchable to the devil. *"We know that anyone born of God does not continue to sin; the One who was born of God keeps them safe, and the evil one cannot harm them"* (1 John 5:18). This is the reality that comes through knowing who we are in Christ and refusing to agree with satan's lies.

OUR WEAPONS

Since lies are what the devil uses to put people into bondage, truth is the tool that God uses to set people free. As the Bible says: *"Then you will know the truth, and the truth will set you free"* (John 8:32).

For us to remain fixed in our triumph over the devil, we must remember two important words: *resist* and *stand*. The devil is already defeated, he has already lost, and there is nothing we can do to add to what Christ accomplished on the cross. So our current strategy is to *resist* and *stand* firm against the devil. We are standing and resisting the devil's lies since they are the only weapons he has left.

> **Resist him, standing firm** in the faith... (1 Peter 5:9).

> ...**Resist the devil,** and he will flee from you (James 4:7).

> Put on the full armor of God so that you can take your **stand against** the devil's schemes....Therefore put on the full armor of God, so that when the day of evil comes, you may be able to **stand your ground,** and after you have done everything, to **stand. Stand firm** then... (Ephesians 6:11;13-14).

According to Ephesians 6, we have one strategy: stand against, stand our ground, stand firm. Once we understand that Jesus has already taken all of the devil's authority, we realize that our objective is not obtaining victory, but maintaining victory. Jesus obtained all authority and then gave it to His followers. Now we are to stand and resist the devil to maintain our position of authority.

Regarding lust, the devil has a whole mess of lies at his disposal. He uses these to trick the Church into not maintaining her freedom and authority. Behind every sexual sin is a lie. Consider the following passage:

> *Therefore God gave them over in the sinful desires of their hearts to sexual impurity for the degrading of their bodies with one another. They exchanged the truth about God for a lie, and worshiped and served created things rather than the Creator—who is forever praised. Amen* (Romans 1:24-25).

Notice what Paul says: they exchanged truth for a lie. This is what led to the sexual impurity mentioned in the verse before. Wherever sexual impurity exists, there is a lie that opened the door. There are literally thousands of lies that the devil has concocted to keep men from walking in their identities and their corresponding authority. We must identify these lies and begin to stand against and resist them with the truth so that we can experience the victory Christ purchased for us.

As long as we continue to believe these lies, we will remain in bondage. If we become aware of the lies that we have agreed with, we can break these agreements, step into the truth, and be set free!

Tool

I recommend carrying a notepad and pen for use with this tool. Whenever you are tempted by lustful thoughts, ask the question, "What lie have I accepted that is allowing this lust to tempt me?"

Begin to write down these lies each time you are tempted. Many times, just seeing the lie on paper disempowers it. Ask the Holy Spirit to tell you what the corresponding truth is regarding the lie. Even if you step into sin, once you have stepped out of it and have repented, use this tool. Begin to capture these lies and hammer them with the truths that the Holy Spirit shows you.

CHAPTER 8

THE LAW

Rather, clothe yourselves with the Lord Jesus Christ, and
do not think about how to gratify the desires of the flesh
—ROMANS 13:14

While traveling and teaching, I share a simple test with many crowds. First, I read the following verse from Job: *"I made a covenant with my eyes not to look lustfully at a young woman"* (Job 31:1). Then I ask the men to raise their hands if they have ever made a similar commitment in their hearts. Without fail, every Christian man will raise his hand. I then ask them to keep their hands up if they have been able to keep this commitment. At that point, they all pull their hands down.

Clearly, men know what is right; they desire to do what is right; they have made countless attempts to do what is right; but they have not been able to succeed. I believe that one of the main reasons why we have not been successful in this arena is that we have been struggling with the wrong tools—*for years.*

If I handed you a hammer, nails, and a screwdriver and asked you to make dinner, you wouldn't have the right tools. After endless frustration, you would eventually give up. And since everyone around you is struggling with the same tools and lack of success—well, you get the idea.

The Old Testament law was a tool to show how powerless we are over sin. The law never gave power over sin; it actually identified, aroused, and empowered sin.

> *When we were controlled by our old* [sinful] *nature, sinful desires were at work within us, and the law aroused these evil desires that produced a harvest of sinful deeds, resulting in death* (Romans 7:5 NLT).

> *The sting of death is sin, and the power of sin is the law* (1 Corinthians 15:56).

> *What shall we say, then? Is the law sin? Certainly not! Nevertheless, I would not have known what sinful was had it not been for the law. For I would not have known what coveting really was if the law had not said, "You shall not covet." But sin, seizing the opportunity afforded by the commandment, produced in me every kind of coveting. For apart from the law, sin was dead. Once I was alive apart from the law; but when the commandment came, sin sprang to life and I died* (Romans 7:7-9).

The main strategy for dealing with sin in the Old Testament is, "Don't." That is what we end up with when we see verses such as, *"I made a covenant with my eyes not to look lustfully at a young woman"* (Job 31:1). Most men are still trying to fight temptation the same way that Job did. I am not giving license for looking lustfully, but I do need to state that *don't* is never going to be a successful strategy. There is a fundamental flaw in this type of approach. Imagine if I were to create a law stating that it is a sin to think of oranges. The obvious directive is: "Don't think of oranges." But instead of helping you to avoid sin, the law *immediately* stirs within you the desire to rebel.

Do the following exercise by reading aloud:

> Don't think of oranges. Don't think of the round baseball-sized fruit in your hand. Don't picture its size and color; don't think of peeling it; don't think about the juice getting all over your hands. Don't think of the citrus smell filling the air; don't think of the segments of fruit as they break apart in your hands.

How well did you do at *not* picturing an orange? Yeah. Not so good, right?

Try this one, say the word *yawn* out loud, but don't yawn. If you are like most readers, you will yawn just at the sight of the word. This is the fascinating power of focus.

I have found that the New Testament contains many powerful revelations, but the one that frees us from focusing on *don't* is *but rather*.

Now if I were to add to the previous exercise:

> Don't think of an orange, but rather think of an elephant. Think of the large, grey beast. Picture how tall it is and how long its trunk is; picture the funny little tail, the four big, tree-like legs and the floppy, leathery ears.

Now were you thinking of an elephant, or were you thinking of an orange? Of course you were thinking of the elephant and not the orange. That is the power of the *but rather* revelation. All throughout the New Testament we find the *but rather* revelation; here are some paraphrased examples:

> *Don't fear man,* **but rather** *fear God* (see Matthew 10:28).

Don't use freedom to wallow in sin, **but rather** *serve one another in love* (see Galatians 5:13).

Don't be obscene, foolish, or coarse, **but rather** *give thanks* (see Ephesians 5:4).

Don't have anything to do with darkness, **but rather** *expose the darkness* (see Ephesians 5:11).

Don't become enslaved to philosophy, **but rather** *follow Christ* (see Colossians 2:8).

Don't get caught up in controversies, **but rather** *focus on God's work* (see 1 Timothy 1:4).

Don't gossip, **but rather** *train yourself to be godly* (see 1 Timothy 4:7).

Don't be sinful, **but rather** *be lovers of God* (see 2 Timothy 3:4).

Don't be disabled, **but rather** *healed* (see Hebrews 12:13).

Don't live for earthly desires, **but rather** *for the will of God* (see 1 Peter 4:2).

Don't be involved in sexual immorality, **but rather** *clothe yourself with Christ* (see Romans 13:14).

I remember reading the story a few years ago of a rock star who accepted the Lord. His name is Brian "Head" Welch, and he was the guitarist of the band Korn. In the interview he responded to and confirmed the rumor that he had a picture of Jesus tattooed to the palm of his hand. He said this was done so that he would stop masturbating. Now I am not suggesting this as a standard method for the rest of us, but Brian has put the *but rather* principle to work in his own hilarious way.

The main principle of *but rather* is that you change from what you shouldn't focus on to whom you should be focusing on. Throughout the New Testament we find that our focus and attention is to be on Heaven and the Lord Jesus Christ. For example:

> *Since, then, you have been raised with Christ, **set your hearts on things above**, where Christ i,s seated at the right hand of God **Set your minds on things above**, not on earthly things. For you died, and your life is now hidden with Christ in God* (Colossians 3:1-3).

> *Therefore, holy brothers and sister,s who share in the heavenly calling, **fix your thoughts on Jesus,** whom we acknowledge as our apostle and high priest* (Hebrews 3:1).

> ***Draw near to God and He will draw near to you.** Cleanse your hands, you sinners; and purify your hearts, you double-minded* (James 4:8 NASB).

> *He* [Moses] *chose to be mistreated along with the people of God rather than to enjoy the fleeting pleasures of sin. He regarded disgrace for the sake of Christ as of greater value than the treasures of Egypt, because he was looking ahead to his reward. By faith he left Egypt, not fearing the king's anger; **he persevered because he saw Him who is invisible*** (Hebrews 11:25-27).

> *[Let us fix] **our eyes on Jesus,** the pioneer and perfecter of faith. For the joy set before Him He endured the cross, scorning its shame, and sat down at the right hand of the throne of God* (Hebrews 12:2).

Those who live according to the flesh have their minds set on what the flesh desires; but those who live in accordance with the Spirit **have their minds set on what the Spirit desires** (Romans 8:5).

Rather, **clothe yourselves with the Lord Jesus Christ,** *and do not think about how to gratify the desires of the flesh* (Romans 13:14).

"For I know the plans I have for you," declares the Lord, "plans to prosper you and not to harm you, plans to give you hope and a future. Then you will call on Me and come and pray to Me, and I will listen to you. **You will seek Me and find Me when you seek Me with all your heart. I will be found by you," declares the Lord, "and will bring you back from captivity.** *I will gather you from all the nations and places where I have banished you," declares the Lord, "and will bring you back to the place from which I carried you into exile"* (Jeremiah 29:11-14).

My eyes are ever on the Lord, *for only He will release my feet from the snare* (Psalm 25:15).

BREAKING PATTERNS

I have found that identifying certain patterns and applying the *but rather* revelation to those patterns has brought about great results. For example, I found that I was often tempted to lust in certain locations— in a bathroom, in a shower, in a hotel room, and so forth. For me to apply the *but rather* revelation, I chose that every time I was in one of those locations, I would focus my heart in prayer for freedom for my sisters in the sex industry. I became proactive; rather than waiting until lust attacked me and I had to defend myself, I chose those places as my new prayer closets for tearing down the devil's kingdom of lust.

The *but rather* revelation has endless applications and must be personalized. Figure out where and how you have been failing to maintain your identity, and ask the Lord how you can be proactive to bring change to those situations. The Lord wants you free even more than you want to be free; in fact, He died for your freedom. He surely will give you creative applications for the *but rather* revelation. If you learn to be self-controlled with your focus, then you will be able maintain your walk of integrity: *"My eyes are ever on the Lord, for only He will release my feet from the snare"* (Psalm 25:15).

Tool

The *but rather* revelation is a powerful tool in your arsenal against sexual temptation. Consider where and how you have been failing to maintain your identity, and ask the Lord how you can be proactive to bring change to those situations. Be proactive in finding and applying solutions for the future. The devil is already preparing to try and tempt you; be one step ahead of him so that you are not caught off guard.

For example, if you are consistently tempted to lust while in the shower, then make the following choice before you step into the shower: "I am dedicating my shower time to pray for those in the sex industry, to pray the prayer from page 141."

You must become proactive in using the *but rather* revelation. If there is a private place in your home where you are frequently tempted, perhaps you could post the prayers from page 141 and pray them through each time that you enter that place. If you are tempted in the shower, then laminate the prayer and post it on the wall.[1]

CHAPTER 9

TEMPTATION

God grants liberty only to those who love it, and
are always ready to guard and defend it.
—Daniel Webster

One day as I was being tempted, I asked the Holy Spirit to reveal to me the lie that I believed in that moment. Here is a synopsis of the conversation that took place in my heart in prayer.

> *Holy Spirit: "The lie you believe is that you are tempted by sexual sin."*
>
> *Jonathan: "Um...yes, I am tempted by sexual sin. That doesn't mean that I want to sin, but aren't I always going to be tempted by sexual sin?"*
>
> *Holy Spirit: "Did I crucify your old flesh nature on the cross in Christ?"*
>
> *Jonathan: "Yes."*
>
> *Holy Spirit: "Did I make you a partaker of the divine nature?"*
>
> *Jonathan: "Yes."*

Holy Spirit: "Knowing that God is never tempted by sin, what part of you is drawn after and tempted by sin?" (See James 1:13.)

Jonathan: "Are you saying that I should never be tempted again?"

Holy Spirit: "Not exactly. Temptation will always come. But because your flesh nature has been replaced by divine nature, there is nothing within you drawn toward sin."

Jonathan: "So temptation will pass in front of me, but I will not be tempted by it?"

Holy Spirit: "Exactly!"

Many have taught that as Christians we will always be tempted by sin; but victory in Christ means that we don't have to give into temptations any longer. While I agree that victory includes not sinning, I would suggest that perhaps we have set our sights too low by accepting the idea that we will continue to feel tempted and drawn toward sin. After this surprising conversation with the Holy Spirit, I reexamined every passage in the New Testament about temptation. In this chapter I will unpack my findings. Some of them are quite surprising.

PEIRAZO

There are five words in the New Testament that share the same Greek root word: *prove, examine, test, trials,* and *temptation* all come from *peirazo* in the Greek.[1] When the translators took *peirazo* and translated it into the English Bible, the main way of determining which of the five English words to use was based on the context. If we do not understand this clearly, then it is easy to create contradictions that are not actually in the text. Unfortunately, in some cases the translators did fail to use the right English word for *peirazo,* and this has caused confusion in how we understand certain passages of the Bible.

For example, we see in the Book of James that God never tempts His creation to sin:

> *Let no one say when he is tempted, "I am tempted by God"; for God cannot be tempted by evil, nor does He Himself tempt anyone* (James 1:13 NKJV).

Yet in the Lord's Prayer, Jesus says to pray that God would not lead us into temptation (see Matt. 6:9-13). Why would we pray that, since James says God never tempts us?

Once we understand that the root word can be translated five different ways, it becomes clear that the Lord's Prayer would be better translated, "lead us not into *trials.*" This is just one clear example of how we must understand the contextual usage of the word *tempt.* Another example would be the many times that the Bible says not to *tempt God;* it would be more accurate to say, "do not *test* God," because James 1:13 says that God cannot be tempted.

Now that we are aware of the different applications of the word *peirazo,* we can begin to clearly differentiate between two very different concepts: *temptation* and *trial.*

TEMPTATION VERSUS TRIAL

The Bible teaches that God handles temptations and trials differently. Trials are processes that we go through, whereas temptations are occurrences and events. When we encounter temptation, God always gives a way of escape, a back door of sorts. Paul and Peter both make this clear:

> *No temptation has overtaken you except such as is common to man; but God is faithful, who will not allow you to be tempted beyond what you are able, but with the temptation **will also make the way of escape,** that you may be able to bear it* (1 Corinthians 10:13 NKJV).

> *...the Lord knows **how to deliver the godly out of tempta-tions** and to reserve the unjust under punishment for the day of judgment* (2 Peter 2:9 NKJV).

In contrast to temptation, when we go through trials, God does *not* always provide a way out. This is why Jesus said to pray that we would not enter into trials. Consider the examples of Jesus and Paul:

> *Father, if You are willing, take this cup from Me; yet not My will, but Yours be done* (Luke 22:42).

> *...I refrain* [from boasting], *so no one will think more of me than is warranted by what I do or say, or because of these surpassingly great revelations. Therefore, in order to keep me from becoming conceited, I was given a thorn in my flesh, a messenger of Satan, to torment me. Three times I pleaded with the Lord to take it away from me. But He said to me, "My grace is sufficient for you, for My power is made perfect in weakness." Therefore I will boast all the more gladly about my weaknesses, so that Christ's power may rest on me. That is why, for Christ's sake, I delight in weaknesses, in insults, in hardships, in persecutions, in difficulties. For when I am weak, then I am strong* (2 Corinthians 12:6-10).

Both Jesus and Paul prayed that God would remove the trials that they were going through. In both cases, God gave them the empowerment needed to continue in the trial, yet He gave them no supernatural escape. Yet with temptation, God does not call us to endure it. He provides a way out! We always have a way out of temptation.

This distinction is very clear in the Word, and it is essential to finding freedom from temptation. If God is putting you through a trial, you can pray that He would deliver you. However, when you face temptation to sin, you do not need to pray for a way of escape; God has already promised a way of escape (see 1 Cor. 10:13).

In *temptation*, satan comes to God like the neighborhood rascal asking your father if you are home. God, your Father, asks "Why?" Satan replies that he has some illegal fireworks and he wants to see if you would like to join him in setting them off.

God your Father knows that you are big enough, wise enough, and well-trained enough that He can trust you with this temptation—knowing that you will say no. God allows temptation because it is a good test for you to prove yourself. He believes that you will win against it every time! Thus, He only allows you to face temptations that you are equipped to overcome—this is your way out!

In *trials,* God is much more intimately involved. I picture Him hovering over us closely as we walk through hardships and pain in our lives. Even if we don't realize it at the moment, we can often look back and see His hand in our trials, because He always walks alongside of us while we go through them. He supplies the grace and strength we need.

God's ultimate goal is to discipline us as sons and release more fruit through our lives. This is what the author of Hebrews wrote of:

> *And have you completely forgotten this word of encouragement that addresses you as a father addresses his son? It says, "My son, do not make light of the Lord's discipline, and do not lose heart when He rebukes you, because the Lord disciplines the one He loves, and He chastens everyone He accepts as His son."*
>
> *Endure hardship as discipline; God is treating you as His children. For what children are not disciplined by their father? If you are not disciplined—and everyone undergoes discipline—then you are not legitimate, not true sons and daughters at all. Moreover, we have all had human fathers who disciplined*

us and we respected them for it. How much more should we submit to the Father of spirits and live! They disciplined us for a little while as they thought best; but God disciplines us for our good, in order that we may share in His holiness. No discipline seems pleasant at the time, but painful. Later on, however, it produces a harvest of righteousness and peace for those who have been trained by it (Hebrews 12:5-11).

The purpose of discipline and trials is that we might share in God's holiness. What an awesome goal! Many people equate discipline with punishment; but God's discipline is training, not punishment. God is literally conforming us into the image of His Son (see Rom. 8:29).

TEMPTATION TEACHES US

I have come to understand that temptation exists merely as a means for us to be *examined* or *proven*. Our temptations are similar to the placing a sword against a grindstone. The grindstone is never meant to damage the blade; it is only meant to sharpen it. In the same way, temptation was provided for our benefit, to sharpen us. We are never to bow to its wishes; but the very existence of temptation provides us with the needed choices to prove our freedom and exercise self-control.

God actually uses temptation to test and prove us. Consider that it was actually the Holy Spirit who drove Jesus into the wilderness so that He would be tempted by the devil:

Immediately the Spirit drove Him into the wilderness. And He was there in the wilderness forty days, tempted by Satan, and was with the wild beasts; and the angels ministered to Him (Mark 1:12-13 NKJV; see also Matthew 4:1-11).

God does not allow temptation to override our free will. Some people say that the temptation they faced was too much and that they had no choice but to sin. This is absolutely not true because "...*God is faithful, who will not allow you to be tempted beyond what you are able...*" (1 Cor. 10:13 NKJV).

But God *will* allow temptation to test our limits. God uses temptation to examine and prove us. He never allows a temptation we cannot succeed in overcoming, and He always provides a way of escape. This whole test is set up with our success in mind; it is slanted in our favor in every possible way!

GOD WANTS TO PROVE YOU *TO YOU*

A temptation is actually a test to show us how powerful we are. In an attempt to prove the true freedom that we have received in Christ, some people have said that temptation is not a sin and that temptation says nothing about our character. This statement is a half-truth. Temptation is not a sin, but it does say volumes about our character. *The bigger the temptation, the more positive of a statement God is speaking about us.* The temptation that we can handle shows the level to which God believes He can trust us.

Considering that there was temptation in the Garden of Eden and that even Jesus was tempted (see Matt. 4:1-11), we know that temptation is not a bad thing. I believe that God's ultimate intention in allowing temptation in our lives is to prove something to us. It's not, as so many have thought, that we are trying to prove something to Him. He doesn't need us to prove ourselves to Him; He is not that insecure. However, He knows that we don't understand what He has done in our lives, so He allows temptation to prove to us how amazing we are.

God wanted both Adam and Jesus to see that they could go toe-to-toe with satan himself and totally defeat temptation. Unfortunately Adam didn't understand this, and he failed. But now we have been made new creations in Christ (see 2 Cor. 5:17). God has set us totally free from the flesh, and He wants to prove this to us. Isn't it just like God to take one of satan's most powerful tools, designed to create shame and condemnation, and use it to prove to us our righteousness in Christ? The truth is, we *are* righteous in Christ. Temptation is not a sin. It is there to prove how free we really are!

ENDING THE INNER STRUGGLE

Here is an important point to grasp: God cannot be tempted to sin *"...for God cannot be tempted by evil, nor does He Himself tempt anyone"* (James 1:13 NKJV). Consider this verse in the light of Jesus' temptation by satan in the wilderness (see Matt. 4). This means that there was nothing in Jesus that actually responded to the temptation. There was no inner struggle or battle for His choices. He carried the divine nature; therefore, as most commentaries show, Jesus didn't have anything in His heart for satan to tempt (see John 14:30).

James says that *"each person is tempted when they are dragged away by their own evil desire and enticed"* (James 1:14). Yet, because Jesus carried God's nature, He could not be tempted to enter into sin. What James wrote is a general truth about the nature of how temptation operates. He was not writing to say that this will be true of the believer's remaining lifetime. That would be a major contradiction of the rest of the Gospel.

Remember with me the Dr. Jekyll and Mr. Hyde analogy in light of James 1:14. Because we no longer have the flesh nature, the only way that temptation can cling to us is if we are wearing Mr. Hyde's clothing. If we choose to keep and wear his garments, temptation will be able to grab a hold of his clothes and drag us away, according to James 1:14.

Now that the old nature has been put to death, we have become *"partakers of the divine nature, having escaped the corruption that is in the world through lust"* (2 Pet. 1:4 NKJV). Just as was true of Jesus, the enemy should find no place in our hearts to pull on. Temptation will continue to come, but its only purpose is to show us that we have become partakers of the divine nature and temptation has no hold on us. Temptation will come merely to prove that we have *"escaped the corruption that is in the world through lust."* Praise God!

John the apostle wrote, *"Love has been perfected among us in this: that we may have boldness in the day of judgment; because as He is, so are we in this world"* (1 John 4:17 NKJV). This verse says, *"as He is* (present tense—currently reigning in Heaven), *so are we in this world."* Jesus is not currently struggling to remain pure from temptations. Therefore, we shouldn't be either. We are partakers of the divine nature and we are seated in heavenly places; as He is, so are we!

Since our flesh has been crucified and laid in a grave, we are no longer in a struggle with it. It is dead and gone. When the voice of temptation arises and sounds similar to our old flesh, it is actually a *lying, evil spirit.* There is nothing in us that can be drawn by satan toward sin.

Vine's Expository Dictionary of the New Testament reiterates this important point. Jesus had temptations presented to Him, but He had nothing in Him to desire the temptations. Consider this verse from Hebrews:

> *Because He Himself suffered when He was tempted, He is able to help those who are being tempted* (Hebrews 2:18).

According to Vine's

> ...the context shows that the temptation was the cause of suffering to Him, and only suffering, not a drawing away to sin...in all the temptations which Christ endured, there was nothing within Him that answered to sin. There was no sinful infirmity in Him.[2]

FINAL OBJECTIONS

Before closing this chapter, I want to address a few objections I have heard regarding a life free from fighting inner temptations. It is well worth taking the time to respond to the most common ones.

Objection #1: The Bible says, *"In your struggle against sin, you have not yet resisted to the point of shedding your blood"* (Heb. 12:4). So aren't Christians destined to struggle against temptations from their sin nature for the rest of their lives?

Answer: The *Jamieson-Fausset-Brown Bible Commentary* says that, regarding this passage, sin "is personified as an adversary."[3] This means that sin is being referred to in a metaphorical sense. Christians resisting the world system or the kingdom of darkness are pictured in this passage as "struggling against sin." This verse is not in reference to the sin nature. That is why the verse continues by saying, *"you have not yet resisted to the point of shedding your blood,"* in reference to the persecution that was taking place against Christians of the first century. This is the general consensus from most Bible commentators.[4]

Objection #2: The Bible says, *"If we claim to be without sin, we deceive ourselves and the truth is not in us"* (1 John 1:8). Doesn't this mean that we all have a sin nature and will always be subject to its temptations?

Answer: As I have previously shown in the "You Are Crucified in Christ" chapter, our sin nature has already died at the cross, been buried in baptism, and was removed from us through circumcision of the heart. Yet, this verse continues to cause confusion for many. The first key for understanding this verse is that we must read it in its context:

> *This is the message we have heard from Him and declare to you: God is light; in Him there is no darkness at all. If we claim to have fellowship with Him and yet walk in the darkness, we lie and do not live out the truth. But if we walk in the light, as He is in the light, we have fellowship with one another, and the blood of Jesus, His Son, purifies us from all sin.*
>
> ***If we claim to be without sin,*** *we deceive ourselves and the truth is not in us.* ***If we confess our sins,*** *He is faithful and*

just and will forgive us our sins and purify us from all unrighteousness. If we claim we have not sinned, we make Him out to be a liar and His word is not in us.

*My dear children, **I write this to you so that you will not sin. But if** anybody does sin, we have an advocate with the Father—Jesus Christ, the Righteous One. He is the atoning sacrifice for our sins, and not only for ours but also for the sins of the whole world* (1 John 1:5–2:2).

In this passage about walking in the light, John contrasts parallel thoughts in verses 8 and 9. In verse 8, John's point is that if someone will not be open and honest about their mistakes, then they live under self-induced deception. Whereas in verse 9, John says that if a person will be open and honest about their mistakes, then they will be forgiven and purified.

John is not writing to say that a believer will never be free from the grip of sin; otherwise, why would he say in 2:1 that, *"I write this to you so that you will not sin"*? John's perspective was that Christians do not have to sin, *but if* they happen to sin, they should be open and honest about it so that they can receive forgiveness and purification.

In conclusion, if you understand that you are the righteousness of God in Christ, you should also understand that you are not destined to struggle against temptation for the rest of your days. The Bible calls that being double-minded. Satan will set up temptation for the rest of your life; but you do not have to *be* tempted again because there is nothing inside of you to be drawn to that temptation. Temptation is meant to prove you *to you.*

Tool

When temptation comes, remember the acronym: WATNOW! (as in, "What now!")

W hen temptation comes your way, stop for a moment.

A im your heart to Father God and begin to praise Him for trusting you with such a temptation.

T hank Him for believing in you.

N otice that God is proving you to you by allowing this type of temptation into your life.

O bserve that you have been made a partaker of the divine nature; therefore, nothing in you desires to follow that temptation.

W inning is why God allowed it in the first place!

CHAPTER 10

SHAME

*The heaviest garment a person can ever
wear is the garment of shame."*
—Jonathan Welton

Many Christians continue to struggle year after year under the shame of their past sins and mistakes. Yes, the Holy Spirit does convict us of sin, but many have continued to beat themselves up for sins that have already been forgiven. The guilt and shame of our mistakes seem to stalk us long after we have been forgiven. Many of us never move from the initial experience of being a *sinner saved by grace* into the more mature life of being a *saint of the Most High*. What most in the Church need is a clear view of how God sees them and how they should be viewing themselves.

I find the story of Sarah to be a great insight into how God views us, both before and after repentance.

> *Then they said to him, "Where is Sarah your wife?"*
> *So he said, "Here, in the tent."*
> *And He said, "I will certainly return to you according to the time of life, and behold, Sarah your wife shall have a son."*

(Sarah was listening in the tent door which was behind him.) Now Abraham and Sarah were old, well advanced in age; and Sarah had passed the age of childbearing. Therefore Sarah laughed within herself, saying, "After I have grown old, shall I have pleasure, my lord being old also?"

And the Lord said to Abraham, "Why did Sarah laugh, saying, 'Shall I surely bear a child, since I am old?' Is anything too hard for the Lord? At the appointed time I will return to you, according to the time of life, and Sarah shall have a son."

But Sarah denied it, saying, "I did not laugh," for she was afraid. And He said, "No, but you did laugh!" (Genesis 18:9-15 NKJV).

This is the historic account of how Sarah responded in the natural. It is important to note that Sarah's laugh, according to the original Hebrew root words in this passage, was a mocking type of laugh. She was not saying, "Oh Lord, You are so funny." She was frustrated and angry toward God, scoffing at His declaration. This is not a response of great faith; it is as far in the opposite direction as you can get. Yet, look at how God remembers this story in the New Testament.

By faith Sarah *herself also received strength to conceive seed, and she bore a child when she was past the age, because she judged Him faithful who had promised. Therefore from one man and him as good as dead, were born as many as the stars of the sky in multitude—innumerable as the sand which is by the seashore* (Hebrews 11:11-12 NKJV).

Just those first three words alone are shocking. In Genesis, Sarah is laughing, mocking, and certainly not full of faith. And then later she conceived a child, and God proved Himself faithful. Somewhere along the way Sarah repented and God rewrote her story.

Fast-forward to the writing of Hebrews, and I can imagine God saying, "OK, this is how I want you to write this down. 'By faith Sarah...'" I wonder if the writer of Hebrews had a hard time writing this, yet this is how the Holy Spirit directed him to record her story. In the eyes of God, repentance literally rewrites the account of our lives.

Like Sarah, when we repent, God changes our history and sets us back on the path of our destiny. If He did not do this, the moment we made our first mistake we would be doomed—to never reaching our destiny. Our sin would have permanently derailed us. Fortunately, *God interacts with us from our destiny, not our history.*

The Past Separates Us

If we do not realize that God changes our history when we repent, we will continue to see ourselves through a reality that, according to God, no longer exists. If He changed our past and we do not make the transition to seeing our past through His eyes, we are submitting ourselves to a false reality. God goes so far as to tell us that the past does not belong to us.

> *So then, no more boasting about human leaders! All things are yours, whether Paul or Apollos or Cephas [Peter] or the world or life or death or the **present or the future**—all are yours, and you are of Christ, and Christ is of God* (1 Corinthians 3:21-23).

All things are ours, including the present and the future, but *the past* is not ours, and that is why He excluded it from the list. Our past does not belong to us; it belongs to God, which is why He can rewrite it as He so chooses. He goes on to tell us that our past can separate us from His love.

> *For I am convinced that neither death nor life, neither angels nor demons, neither the **present nor the future**, nor any*

powers, neither height nor depth, nor anything else in all creation, will be able to separate us from the love of God that is in Christ Jesus our Lord (Romans 8:38-39).

Most people read this verse and go on to conclude that nothing can separate us from the love of God. I would contend that *the past* was left off that list on purpose, because it *will* separate us from the love of God. God does not separate Himself from us, but when we access our past, we choose to turn away from Him. Because God does not exist in our repented-of past, we literally have to leave God behind when we choose to dwell there. By looking back in time, we turn away from Him and our future, which is where He already is.

God does not want us to access our past apart from His rewriting of it. When we rehearse the past, we open the opportunity to repeat it. It is easy to fall into a cycle of repetition because the past (which our repentance changed) does not lead us to our destiny. Let me repeat: The repented-of past actually does not exist; therefore, to go back there is to live in a false reality that leads to a false present and a false future.

The danger of rehearsing the past is the same one that the ancient heroes and heroines of faith had to avoid:

All these people were still living by faith when they died. They did not receive the things promised; they only saw them and welcomed them from a distance, admitting that they were foreigners and strangers on earth. People who say such things show that they are looking for a country of their own. ***If they had been thinking of the country they had left, they would have had opportunity to return. Instead, they were longing for a better country—a heavenly one.*** *Therefore God is not ashamed to be called their God, for He has prepared a city for them* (Hebrews 11:13-16).

If these men and women had focused on the past, they would have found themselves repeating it. The problem is not the content of the past, but rather, our focus. We all tend to head toward where we focus, and as the old saying goes: *If you don't change your direction, you will end up where you are headed.*

Hebrews 11:16 says that *"God is not ashamed to be called their God...."* This is not because they had a spotless past. God is not ashamed because they did not make the past their focus. It would have put God to shame if, after He had forgiven them, they chose to go back and rehearse the past over and over. That would have demonstrated a total disregard for God's forgiveness; it would have shown no desire to move forward with Him. Instead, they closed the door on the past. Their focus was not on what was *behind* the door; their focus was on *closing* the door.

Hebrews 11 shows us that making mistakes is forgivable. As long as our failings are put in the past, they do not shame God. But when we keep ourselves living in and from the past, we never move forward.

Consider this amazing reality: God does not choose to forgive us when we repent; He chose to forgive us 2,000 years ago. *Before we were born, we were completely forgiven.*

Thus, the purpose of repentance is not pleading with or convincing God to forgive a particular sin; He has already provided forgiveness for us. Likewise, God does not show us our sins to demand an apology, but so that we can see those sins for what they are and the harm they cause. When we see this, we will repent and turn away from it. When we repent, we turn our heart back to Him so we can receive His forgiveness. Once we have received the forgiveness He already purchased for us, there is no more need for repentance.

Many have said that the Old Testament was *works-based salvation* and that the New Testament is *grace-based salvation*. The truth is that faith has always been the only way to righteousness in both the Old and New Testaments. *"For it is by grace you have been saved, through faith..."* (Eph. 2:8).

In the Old Testament, animal sacrifices were performed not as *works*, but in faith as a proclamation looking forward to the day of Jesus' sacrifice (see Heb 8:5; Col. 2:16-17). The Old Testament saints believed *toward* a coming Messiah, whereas New Testament saints believe *back toward* the completed work of the Messiah. In both cases, it is a matter of faith, because people in both eras receive by faith from the same event in history: Jesus' death on the cross in A.D. 33.

Before we were born, before we sinned, and before we repented, Jesus had already provided forgiveness for us on the cross 2,000 years ago. *"He is the atoning sacrifice for our sins, and not only for ours but also for the sins of the whole world"* (1 John 2:2). Jesus died not only for our sins, but also for every sin ever committed. God has chosen to forgive all sin for all time. So now we must make the choice to receive His forgiveness by faith.

Like a steel cable of forgiveness suspended throughout all of eternity, Jesus' shed blood runs through the whole timeline infinitely in both directions. He established forgiveness for all sin before any humans were even created and made it accessible by faith. Jesus was *"the Lamb who was slain from the creation of the world"* (Rev. 13:8). All that one must do to receive forgiveness is reach out and grasp it by faith.[1]

PRE-FORGIVEN

Imagine with me a man named Joe. In 1980, Joe accepted Jesus as his Savior. When Joe repented of his sins, Jesus had already forgiven Joe at the cross (in A.D. 33); but God's forgiveness was not applied to Joe until Joe received it by faith. In essence, Joe reached out into eternity and grasped the steel cable of forgiveness and pulled it into 1980. Jesus did not decide to forgive Joe in 1980. Jesus decided to forgive

Joe before the creation of the world (see Rev. 13:8). However, salvation occurred only when Joe understood and grasped his forgiveness by faith.

Unfortunately, many Christians think that every time they sin, God must choose to forgive them again. Some have reached the point where they do not even want to ask forgiveness again because they have repented hundreds of times previously. This mindset has led to the feeling that they have to convince God to forgive them once more, in the hope that perhaps this time they will not sin again. It is as though they feel like God must be tired of choosing to forgive them again and again. Or the thought may be: *If I were God, I would have stopped forgiving me by now!*

The truth is that God made one choice to forgive all sin forever. Therefore, He never has to choose to forgive again. To put it another way, we have been *pre-forgiven* for anything and everything we could ever do. When we sin, we are not coming to God to *ask* Him to forgive us. He already has! We are coming to God to *receive* His forgiveness by faith. *"And by* [His] *will, we have been made holy through the sacrifice of the body of Jesus Christ once for all"* (Heb. 10:10).

GOD CONFRONTS FOR OUR SAKES

Even when God confronts us and convicts us of our sin, it is for our benefit. In human relationships, many confrontations are approached with a demand that the violator must apologize enough to earn forgiveness. However, when God comes to address us, He has already forgiven us; He is coming not to demand an apology, but to show us our sin so that we stop. That's why God reveals our sin to us. He doesn't get so much out of it compared to the fact that we get everything out of it.

In human relationships, typically the only time that we hear about our sin is when someone has been hurt and is demanding an apology.

Yet with God, He forgives us and *then* He confronts us. So by the time God confronts us, it is actually for our benefit and for restored or improved relationship with Him.

Once God confronts us about our sin, the repentance He desires from us is not a matter of epic tears, but of a change of direction. True change is not brought about from condemnation and guilt, but from a loving and forgiving Father. He comes to show us the destruction of our ways. It is *"the kindness of God* [which] *leads* [us] *to repentance..."* (Rom. 2:4 NASB).

We do not have to convince God to forgive us because He already has. We need to accept the fact of His complete forgiveness before we sinned, during our sins, and after we sinned. If we sin, we do not need to convince God that we are worthy of a second chance. *We have been preemptively forgiven* for anything we could ever do. Jesus' death provided a perfect sacrifice so that all our sins could be covered once for all time (see 1 Pet. 3:18; Rom. 6:10; Heb. 7:27; 10:10). We must continue to receive our forgiveness by faith.

CONVICTION VERSUS CONDEMNATION

Many of us have been taught that we should remember our failures so that we can learn from them. As we have learned in the previous chapter, this is not how the Kingdom of God operates. The Lord desires that we leave the past behind, not that we focus on it and try not to repeat it.

Many have tried to live under a cloud of condemnation because they equate *awareness of sin* with *holiness*. This is a tremendous lie from satan. If we do not close the door to the past, *condemnation* will destroy our confidence in Christ's forgiveness.

What is condemnation? *Merriam-Webster* says that *to condemn* is "to declare to be reprehensible, wrong or evil, usually after weighing evidence and without reservation...to pronounce guilty...to adjudge unfit for use..."[2] Some of the synonyms are, "to criticize, to sentence or to doom."[3]

Regarding those who have repented and received forgiveness by faith, the Bible says, *"Therefore, there is now no condemnation for those who are in Christ Jesus..."* (Rom. 8:1). God is not sitting in Heaven criticizing us, passing sentence on us, placing doom on us, or saying we are unfit for use, guilty without reservation, or reprehensible. God the Father never condemns His children. There is no condemnation in Christ.

Condemnation is a tool that satan tries to use against believers. If, after you have repented, you continue to hear words in your heart declaring your guilt, you are hearing satan's voice of condemnation. At that point, it is best to command the voice of the demonic to be silent. The Lord never uses condemnation to correct His children. He uses the much gentler voice of conviction.

Conviction is defined by *Webster's* as "...the act of convincing" or "...the state of being convinced."[4] It is the job of the Holy Spirit to convince you when you have committed a sin. It is not His job to beat you and make you feel terrible.

Most of us know that the Holy Spirit convicts us of sin. However, most Christians do not realize that the Holy Spirit actually convicts us of three different things. Jesus told His disciples: *"And He, when He comes, will convict the world regarding* [1] *sin and* [2] *righteousness and* [3] *judgment"* (John 16:8 NASB).

CONVICTION OF SIN

The Holy Spirit convinces our hearts that we have committed a sin or sins. We should then repent to God and (when applicable) to the person whom we hurt so that relationship can be restored.

We discern conviction of sin, as opposed to condemnation, because the Holy Spirit's voice is always going to come through love. God is love, and He always speaks the truth in love. We must reject any voice we hear in our hearts saying, *"I cannot believe that you are a Christian by the way that you have been acting. You sicken me; you are despicable; you are reprehensible; you should be ashamed."* That is not a voice from Heaven, but from the enemy.

CONVICTION OF RIGHTEOUSNESS

Once the Holy Spirit has convinced us of error and we have repented, He then begins to convince us of our righteousness. He says things like, *"You are better than this; this is not who you are. I have read the end of your story. You are a mighty man of God, not a coward. You are the righteousness of God in Christ. Now, stand up tall; walk with confidence; walk in love; walk in strength. I have called you to holiness."*

This is the voice of the Holy Spirit convincing us of our righteousness in Christ Jesus.

CONVICTION OF JUDGMENT

Finally, the Holy Spirit convinces us to exact retribution upon the kingdom of darkness. This is not about judgment toward our sin. Our judgment was removed when we repented of our sin. In fact, verse 11 of John 16 goes on to explain that the conviction of judgment is in regard to satan: *"and concerning judgment, because the ruler of this world has been judged."*

First, the Holy Spirit convicts people of their sin. Second (after they repent), He convicts them of their righteous standing with God. Third, conviction from the Holy Spirit reassigns them to exact retribution on the tempting spirits that mislead them from the path of righteousness—He sends them to destroy the works of the enemy!

This is how God brings punishment upon satan. Once we are free from the very things that kept us bound, perhaps even for years—whether lust, bitterness, shame, alcoholism, whatever—we are sent out to expose and crush these same works of darkness. *The chains that bound us are given back to us for the whipping of the enemy.*

Condemnation is demonic, whereas conviction is heavenly. Conviction brings a momentary awareness of sin; then once we have repented, conviction tells us how Christ chooses to see us, and sends us out to bring judgment upon the devil. Once we understand this amazing truth, we will begin to see that conviction is awesome, wonderful, cleansing, and sometimes even fun.

Picture a small boy named Timmy. One day Timmy is caught pushing his sister to the ground, and his mom rebukes him, telling him that pushing his sister is wrong. Timmy is convicted and quickly apologizes to his mom and sister for his actions. Then his mom pulls him close and tells him, "Timmy, you are a powerful man of God; you are a man full of respect and honor. You are not the type of boy who pushes little girls; you are the kind of boy that protects little girls. Do you understand?"

"Yes'um," Timmy says.

"Timmy," says mom, "from here forward I am commissioning you to be your little sister's protector. You are called to guard her and watch over her. Make sure that she is always treated with respect, honor, and kindness. Can you do that?"

"Oh boy!" Timmy replies, "I sure can!"

This story illustrates exactly what God does with His three-step conviction process. We must not narrow down our understanding of conviction to merely becoming aware of sin. Parts two and three of conviction are life-giving, empowering, and fun.

Recently, I was faced with a situation where I was reminded of the power of full conviction (sin/righteousness/judgment). I was sitting in the hot tub at my gym, which is in a very public setting, when a beautiful young lady came and sat in the tub across from me. At first I felt a bit awkward; then the vile thoughts came. One after another, awful ideas filled my mind. After a few moments of hopelessly fighting them off, I felt the Holy Spirit convict me regarding the sinful nature of the things crossing my mind. I came into agreement with Him and repented for allowing them at all. Then I sat and listened as the Holy Spirit spoke to my heart.

"Jonathan, you are a man of God. You don't see women that way. They are your sisters, and you are filled with love, honor, and respect for them." After a few minutes of the Holy Spirit convicting me of my righteousness, my identity and confidence were restored. My awkwardness also left me. I was able to look that beautiful young lady in the face without those distracting thoughts because I remembered who I was (and am). The Holy Spirit went on to convict me of judgment regarding the devil and showed me how to bring retribution.

He said, "Jonathan, you are called as a protector of beauty—whether in nature, infants, art, health, or this young lady—I have called you as a protector of beauty. I want you to begin to pray protection over her. Release the love of Father God over her and pray into her destiny." As I sat there praying for her in my heart, I began to feel God's love for her. In a matter of minutes, I had moved from a helpless victim with a mind full of temptation into a powerful man filled with the heart of God toward the woman.

I actually got the impression that God had destined her to do something with photography. I introduced myself and told her that I was a Christian author and that sometimes when I pray, God tells me about other people. And with that I told her about the impression I had about her destiny in photography. This tremendously blessed her because she had actually done some modeling and wasn't feeling very confident about which direction to go with her life.

I have come to realize that many times when the devil brings lustful thoughts into my mind, the Lord is actually setting me up for a divine appointment that will be fulfilled if I will recognize it and come into alignment with the Holy Spirit. Full conviction takes the whip out of our enemy's hands, puts us back on our feet, and puts the whip in our hands!

A CLEAN CONSCIENCE

Even though we have been forgiven, when we sin, we violate part of our human spirit called the *conscience*. The conscience is a spiritual organ within us that the Holy Spirit speaks to when He convicts us of sin. Our sin stains our conscience, and only blood can cleanse this stain. Thus, we must choose to draw near to God to receive cleansing from the guilty conscience.

> ***Let us draw near to God*** *with a sincere heart and with the full assurance that faith brings, having our hearts sprinkled to* ***cleanse us from a guilty conscience*** *and having our bodies washed with pure water* (Hebrews 10:22).

In the Old Testament, the blood of the animal sacrifice did not have power to cleanse the conscience. Animal sacrifice done in faith connected people to forgiveness, making them right with God, but it did nothing to cleanse the conscience of the individual who had sinned. Speaking of the Old Testament sacrificial system, it says in Hebrews:

> *This is an illustration for the present time, indicating that the gifts and sacrifices being offered* ***were not able to clear the conscience*** *of the worshiper* (Hebrews 9:9).

> *The law is only a shadow of the good things that are coming—not the realities themselves. For this reason it can never, by the same sacrifices repeated endlessly year after year, make perfect those who draw near to worship. Otherwise, would they not have stopped being offered?* ***For the worshipers would have been cleansed once for all, and would no longer have***

felt guilty for their sins. But those sacrifices are an annual reminder of sins. It is impossible for the blood of bulls and goats to take away sins (Hebrews 10:1-4).

*The blood of goats and bulls and the ashes of a heifer sprinkled on those who are ceremonially unclean sanctify them **so that they are outwardly clean*** (Hebrews 9:13).

We see from these verses that, in the Old Testament, the animal sacrifice only made a person outwardly clean. This left the conscience unrelieved of the pain of sin and failure. As Hebrews 10:3 says, although the Old Testament people were forgiven, they still felt guilty for their sins. In the New Testament, Jesus placed His blood on the conscience so that we can be free from the guilt of our failures:

*How much more, then, **will the blood of Christ, who through the eternal Spirit offered Himself unblemished to God, cleanse our consciences from acts that lead to death**, so that we may serve the living God!* (Hebrews 9:14)

Once Jesus shed His blood, we were not only forgiven, but our conscience could be cleansed from the guilt and shame of failure. Jesus' blood provided forgiveness once for all sin. However, the human conscience becomes defiled over and over again as we sin in life. His cleansing of the conscience was not once for all; rather, it is in an ongoing process of being cleansed each time we stain the conscience by sinning.

The normal state of the conscience for the Christian is the absence of all guilt, sin, and conviction, as Scripture shows:

*The goal of this command is love, which comes from a pure heart and a **good conscience** and a sincere faith* (1 Timothy 1:5).

*I thank God, whom I serve, as my ancestors did, with a **clear conscience**, as night and day I constantly remember you in my prayers* (2 Timothy 1:3).

They [deacons or bishops] *must keep hold of the deep truths of the faith with a **clear conscience*** (1 Timothy 3:9).

But cleansing the conscience is not just a matter of seeking forgiveness. Forgiveness is received by faith; cleansing comes from applying the blood of Jesus to the conscience. For example, when we commit sin, we should approach the Lord this way:

1. *God, I repent of _____* (insert the sinful action).
2. *By faith I receive Your forgiveness.*
3. *Lord, I have defiled my conscience, and I ask that You would sprinkle Your blood upon me for cleansing.*

According to Hebrews 10:22, when our consciences are defiled, they are cleansed by the sprinkling of His blood upon them. We receive His forgiveness by faith, but we must also by faith apply His blood to our hearts to cleanse our conscience.

DEALING WITH MEMORIES

So far we have seen in the Word that God has forgiven all of our sins, past, present, and future, and that Jesus' blood can cleanse the defiled conscience. However, there may be many past sexual experiences that have left shame in our memories. We must address these memories specifically because, even though we have been forgiven and the Lord has rewritten our past, the devil uses our memories against us. He works to bind us to the shame in these memories to keep us from standing in a clean conscience.

Consider this: We will have our memories in Heaven, but there will be no pain or shame attached to them. Jesus said that life should be *"on earth as it is in heaven"* (Matt. 6:10). If it is to be on Earth as it is in Heaven, then we can have the shame and pain of our memories removed here on Earth. We do not have to wait until Heaven to have our memories healed. In fact, Jesus will transform past experiences from hindrances into testimonies. There is no need to wait until Heaven; we can have our memories changed right now!

Many books have been written on the subject of how to heal memories and bring health to our emotional lives. Unfortunately, many of these books complicate the process of healing until we are left reading something the size of a telephone book. These complex models cannot be found in the ministry of Jesus; therefore, I do not want them. What *is* found in the ministry of Jesus is simply forgiving others. Forgiveness is the profound truth that brings healing to the heart, mind, and memories. (We will see how below.)

If we do not deal with the shame in our memories, we leave ourselves vulnerable to spiritual attack. The apostle Paul spoke of the condition of our hearts when he said, *"...do not give the devil a foothold"* (Eph. 4:27). The picture here is of the heart as a rock-face cliff with places for a climber (satan) to grasp onto. When we allow shame to dwell in our hearts, we give satan something he can work with.

Jesus is our example for all issues in life. Looking at His life, we can see that He gave satan no footholds, nothing to grab onto. He told His disciples as much when He told them, *"I will not say much more to you, for the prince of this world is coming. He has no hold over Me"* (John 14:30).

From what Jesus said, I imagine the clean perfection of His heart: a rock-faced cliff that has been sanded perfectly smooth and covered with petroleum jelly just for good measure.

We too can have clean, smooth hearts, simply by following God's Word. For memories with painful emotions attached to them (such as shame, anger, fear, or hatred), use the following four-step process to pray them through. It is a simple way to address difficult memories and remove any footholds from your heart.

1. *Forgive the offender in detail for what caused the shame or pain.*

2. *Repent for allowing shame, bitterness, and resentment to take root in your heart.*

Step two is more important than most people realize. At some point, each of us has to take responsibility for our own thoughts and feelings. We must realize that we don't just need to forgive others, but God also requires that *we repent* for the putrid resentments in our own souls. Yes, our offenders hurt us, but we were the ones who chose to hold onto those hurts rather than forgive the offense.

3. *Command the lies of the past and the demonic to be silent.*

John 10:5 says: *"They will never follow a stranger; in fact, they will run away from him because they do not recognize a stranger's voice."* Because we are in Christ and shame is not in Him, our shame represents the voice of a stranger. Even though it "sounds" familiar, it is actually a lie because it contradicts what God says: the past no longer exists. So when any lie or any demonic voice of shame attempts to influence our thinking, we must use our authority and command it to be silent.

4. *Ask the Holy Spirit to speak His truth into your heart regarding the memory.*

You may hear a word, a sentence, or perhaps see a picture in your mind. God speaks to people in many different ways. Sometimes when you finish one prayer, the Lord will speak to you about another memory that has shame in it so you can continue your healing process. Many times multiple prayers are needed to bring total healing to the affected memories. Pain is an excellent guidepost; keep praying until all the pain has been removed.

Write down what you hear the Holy Spirit speak to your heart regarding each memory. You will be blessed to be able to go back and read that again in the future. Repeat the four steps for each memory that has pain and shame attached to it.

These four steps are not complicated, but preparation is key. Begin your four-step process by asking the Holy Spirit to show you the memories of shame that are lodged in your heart. Write down whatever He reveals. Then use the four-step process with each memory on your list. Here is a simple prayer example for you to follow as you work through your memories:

> *Father, I choose to forgive* _____ *(insert name) for what he/she did (or said) to me (be specific).*
>
> *I repent for holding unforgiveness toward* _____ *(insert name); I choose to release him/her of his/her debt to me right now. He/she owes me nothing. I repent for believing the lie that I* _____ *(describe the lie).*
>
> *I command the voice of the enemy to be silent. Satan, I will not allow you to speak to me through this memory any longer.*
>
> *Holy Spirit, please tell me Your truth about this memory.*

Now listen to the Holy Spirit.

When I used this four-step process, I spent a week writing my list. Then I went to the local park and sat at a picnic table for two solid hours by myself and prayed through item after item on my list. When I picked up my list to continue after a lunch break, I was surprised to notice a marked difference between the items I had prayed through and the ones I had not. I felt nothing when I looked at the list of the former: no regret, no pain, and no shame. But, when I looked at the items not yet prayed through, I could feel a sting of emotions. That definitely motivated me to finish my list.

A remarkable thing happened when I reached the bottom of my prayer list. I felt as though a large, invisible hand lifted off me. This was the feeling associated with all the pressure and power of the memories that had compelled me to act and think in certain ways. I actually had a hard time standing when that pressure first lifted off because I felt lighter and freer than ever before.

As the week went on, I realized that I was free of the compulsions toward which my memories had been pushing me. Then the Holy Spirit told me that, for the first time, I would begin to understand what true self-control was. Because I had been under the control of my painful memories for so long, I had no idea what *self*-control looked like.

This is *your* time to get free from the pain and lies that hold you in bondage. I encourage you to take your time creating a detailed list; do not rush through the four-step prayer process. It took years to accumulate those painful memories; you can take a few days to heal them.

Healthy Christians are not filled with insecurity about their relationship with God. They know they have been fully forgiven and they know that if they commit a sin, they can immediately receive cleansing from the blood of Jesus sprinkled on their consciences. They have no question about whether or not God will forgive; that issue was settled with the death of Jesus.

No wonder healthy Christians are the most peaceful, confident, calm, tranquil, and secure individuals in the world. They know that they are clean, forgiven, and free of their debt of sin. Healthy Christians have no condemnation, are full of forgiveness, have a clean conscience, and carry no painful memories. Therefore, they walk in confidence and freedom every day.

Tool 1

1. Ask the Holy Spirit to convict you of sin (see John 16:8-9).

2. Repent and ask the Spirit to apply the blood of Jesus to
    your defiled conscience (see Heb. 10:22).

3. Ask the Spirit to remind you of your tremendous righ-
    teousness in Christ (see Rom. 5:17).

4. Let the Spirit redirect your heart toward retribution on
    the demonic (see Rom. 16:19).

Tool 2

1. Create your painful memories list.

2. Use the four-step process, in detail, to address
    each memory.

3. Write down whatever the Holy Spirit says or shows you
    regarding each memory.

(It can be very helpful to have another person read this chapter and
then lead you in prayer through the four-step process.)

SECTION 2 SUMMARY

The devil is a completely defeated foe. His only remaining weapon is his tongue. He uses lies to convince us that he is still powerful and that we are weak. It is time to step into triumph and walk in the truth that sets us free.

Living by the law actually empowers sin. Thankfully, God has given us a new way; we obey the law not by focusing on it, but by focusing on the things God directs us to focus on. No longer do we pursue lust, but rather, we clothe ourselves in Christ, our true identity.

Temptation equals trust. God trusts that we will handle temptation correctly; therefore, He allows temptation to show us who we are as new creations. Temptation is used to prove us to ourselves. Temptation is a compliment from God. He only sets us up for success and never failure.

God has designed us to have a clean conscience and has provided the sprinkled blood of Jesus to cleanse us if we fail. Shame, guilt, and condemnation are completely worthless and unnecessary.

SECTION 3

WHO IS SHE?

Is there a way to view women, not as the enemy of purity, but actually as our sisters and coheirs of the Kingdom of God? Can we appreciate their beauty without stepping into impure thoughts? How should we perceive and relate to women in a way that is honoring to God? Is there such a thing as a slut, whore, or home-wrecker? Or are they all hurting sisters who need our compassion and love? What should the Church do to stem the culture of lust? We can no longer afford to stand idly by while the world is inundated with abuse and filth. We must arise in love and Christlikeness.

CHAPTER 11

SHE IS YOUR SISTER

Treat...younger women as sisters, with absolute purity.
—1 TIMOTHY 5:1-2

Imagine for a moment a typical college man. Let's call him Bill. Bill is into the college social scene. He sees himself as a skin-wrapped package of salivary glands, taste buds, and sex drives. So how does Bill occupy his time with this self-perception? By eating and chasing girls. He eats anything and everything in sight, regardless of its nutritional value. He chases just about anything in a skirt, but he has a special gleam in his eye for luscious-looking Susie, the cheerleader.

> Bill was chasing sweet little Susie around the campus one day when the track coach noticed him. "Hey, this kid can really run!" When the coach finally caught up with Bill he said, "Why don't you come out for the track team?"
>
> "Naw," Bill answered, watching for Susie out of the corner of his eye. "I'm too busy."

But the coach wasn't about to take "naw" for an answer. He finally convinced Bill at least to give track a try.

So Bill started working out with the track team and discovered that he really could run. He changed his eating and sleeping habits and his skills improved further. He started winning some races and posting some excellent times for his event.

Finally, Bill was invited to the big race at the state tournament. He arrived at the track early to stretch and warm up. Then, only a few minutes before his event, guess who showed up: sweet little Susie, looking more beautiful and desirable than ever. She pranced up to Bill in a scanty outfit that accentuated her finer physical features. In her hands was a sumptuous slice of apple pie with several scoops of ice cream piled on the top of it.

"I've missed you, Bill," she sang sweetly. "If you come with me now, you can have all this and me too."

"No way, Susie," Bill responded.

"Why not?" Susie pouted.

"Because I'm a runner."

What is different about Bill? What happened to his drives and glands? He is still the same guy who could pack away three burgers, two bags of fries and a quart of Pepsi without batting an eye. He is still the same guy who was just itching to get close to beautiful Susie. His understanding of himself has changed, though. He no longer sees himself primarily as a bundle of physical urges, but as a disciplined runner. He came to the tournament to run a race. That was his purpose, and Susie's suggestion was at cross-purposes with why he was there and how he perceived himself.[1]

This story from Neil Anderson's book, *Victory Over the Darkness,* shows the power of what the apostle Paul called, *"...being transformed by the renewing of your mind..."* (Rom. 12:2). As we have previously discussed, the current methodologies for dealing with sexual bondage have been unsuccessful. Not only do these methods have faulty foundations, but they also have faulty end-goals.

For many men, if they could be freed of the lustful thoughts that grip their minds and walk uprightly, they would be thrilled. Yet this stops far short of God's desire. God's ultimate aim is not just that we stop lusting, but that He conforms us into the image of His Son (see Rom. 8:29). He plans on making us just like Jesus. *"Those who say they live in God should live their lives as Jesus did"* (1 John 2:6 NLT).

God is not simply focused on getting men to stop masturbating; His goal is that we would be just like Jesus. It is with this in mind that we must renew our minds to have the same goal as God. If we are to be like Jesus, we must examine how Jesus viewed women. Jesus treated all women as sisters or as mothers. Remember how Jesus graciously spoke with the woman at the well in John 4? Even though she had a negative sexual reputation in that region, Jesus spoke so kindly to her that she brought the whole town out to meet Him. Jesus did not run away from her because she was too sexual and tempting. He instead approached her with a heart of love, honor, and compassion, knowing that this precious woman was made in the image of God. (This is exactly how the Holy Spirit moved me to interact with the woman in the gym in Chapter 10.)

Every woman has been created in the image of God and, therefore, is worthy of love, honor, and respect. The apostle Paul told Timothy to treat older women as mothers and younger women as sisters. This is not only applicable to women inside the Church. This is the same type of respect that we must exercise at all times toward all women.

Do not rebuke an older man harshly, but exhort him as if he were your father. Treat younger men as brothers, older women as mothers, and younger women as sisters, with absolute purity (1 Timothy 5:1-2).

I would go so far as to say that there is no such thing as a whore, slut, or prostitute. Although some women may consider themselves to be these people and even live that way, Jesus interacted with everyone on the basis of their creation.

All women were created in the image of God and, therefore, deserve love, honor, and respect. These women are our sisters or our mothers and should be viewed accordingly (even when they don't see themselves correctly).

In a natural, healthy family, it is never acceptable to sexually violate your sister or mother. According to Paul, all women are either "my sister or my mother," and incest is unacceptable in the family of God. (The obvious exception is when we marry; these women become our wives, and the paradigm shifts.) When the mind is renewed to perceive all women as either our sisters or our mothers, then sexual immorality will cease being the major problem it has been.

Consider the following scenario. You are watching a movie and the lead actress begins to disrobe for a sex scene. How do you respond? Do you simply shield your eyes and try not to be tempted, or does your heart fill with compassion toward your sister created in the image of God because she is about to defile herself? Does your heart break for your sister and all the pain that she must be in that she would allow herself to be used in such vile ways? Do you focus on trying not to be tempted, or does a spirit of prayer rise up within you as you cry out for the healing of your sister? (It is also important to mention that I do not condone watching movies where women are disrobing, yet many can relate to the question of how to respond in this situation.)

Perhaps you are going through the checkout at the grocery store and the magazine covers are splashed with lewd photos of women. Are you trying to fight off the tempting thoughts, or has your mind been renewed to being like Christ's? If your mind has been renewed, then you would not be focused on yourself and the temptation. You would be focused on the heart of God, which aches for His daughters (your sisters) who are being injured and defiled. With a renewed mind you see those cover models as your sisters, and your heart breaks for them. They are not the enemy that is tempting you, and you are not in a fight with them.

If we can begin to see women as sisters who are being abused, hurt, harmed, kidnapped, and killed by the sex industry worldwide, we would see that the issue is not just whether we masturbate or not. Masturbating is selfish, but trying to stop lusting solely for the purpose of our own freedom can also be selfish. The issue is that either we are working with God to bring those women into freedom, or we are participating with the demonic spirits who are running the annual $57 billion sex trade. If we are to truly align ourselves with the heart of God and live like Jesus, then whenever temptation rears its head, we will not simply try to avoid sin, but we will begin to cry out for our sisters in bondage.

Many Christian authors who have written about men's sexual purity speak of women in a negative tone. They state that the Christian man is in a battle against all those tempting women out there. Although that may be how it feels at times, it is never the truth. This is actually an inferior understanding. The ultimate truth is that we are powerful and called to be like Christ. Women are not the enemy; women are our sisters, and they need our help.

Have you ever considered that those women who are tempting you are in just as much bondage to sexual sin as you are? And whether you can hear them voice it or not, they desperately want their freedom and healing as well.

I would like to suggest something better than men gathering in dank church basements and declaring that they are sex addicts week after week. How about if a group of men struggling with sexual bondage started to meet across the street from a strip club and cry out in prayer on a weekly basis, praying for their sisters in bondage? Those dear women are lost in darkness; they don't know that God loves them. They feel too hated and dirty to come to church, and they need our prayers. And in the process of meeting to pray for those sisters, God's heart of love for those women would transform the men themselves.

Those women are not the enemy. Porn stars, prostitutes, and strippers are your sisters, and they are hurting. They don't just need Christian men to stop looking at them; they need Christian men to cry out in prayer for them. When was the last time that you heard a Christian leader call people to pray for these dear sisters? I have spent 28 years in church, and never have I heard a leader pray over them. Perhaps the reason that the Church has been failing so badly in the battle against sexual temptation is because we have been living on the defensive rather than aligning with the heart of God, living on the offensive, and becoming prayer warriors and protective brothers. This is a call to arms; we must live on the offensive and not the defensive.

God intends for you to be just like Jesus, but satan intends for you to be just like him. While satan wants you to see your sisters as mere objects of pleasure, God wants you to see them as your sisters. You are called as the protective brother who will cry out in prayer and come to their rescue. Satan wants your eyes to be filled with burning lust. God intends for you to be just like Jesus and to have fire in your eyes, so that you would burn with eyes of love.

I turned around to see the voice that was speaking to me. And when I turned I saw seven golden lampstands, and among the *lampstands was someone like a son of man, dressed in a robe reaching down to His feet and with a golden sash around His chest. The hair on His head was white like wool, as white as snow, and **His eyes were like blazing fire.** His feet were like bronze glowing in a furnace, and His voice was like the sound of rushing waters. In His right hand He held seven stars, and coming out of His mouth was a sharp, double-edged sword. His face was like the sun shining in all its brilliance* (Revelation 1:12-16).

This is the picture that the Scripture gives us of Jesus *after* His resurrection—as He is in His victory. And as we already discussed, John, the man who also saw and recorded this revelation of Jesus, wrote: *"Love has been perfected among us in this: that we may have boldness in the day of judgment; because as He is, so are we in this world"* (1 John 4:17 NKJV). We are called to be just like Jesus; as He is, so are we in this world! His eyes of love burn with the fire of Heaven. Thus, our eyes are meant to burn with love just like His!

The battle with sexual sin has been lost because we have been exchanging one selfish focus for another. The Church has traded the selfish focus of lust for a self-focused search for personal freedom. Personal freedom will be found when we focus on freedom for others.

When you see a beautiful and possibly tempting woman, immediately switch your focus to praying protection over her. Don't turn inward and battle temptation; turn outward and place yourself in prayer as a protector. This identity shift will renew your mind and bring personal freedom as an inadvertent by-product.

Let me illustrate what I am talking about. You are at the mall with your friends, and it seems like everywhere you look you see beautiful women dressed in overly sexualized outfits.

Basically there are two ways for you to respond:

Option #1: You feel your conscience begin to condemn you, so you immediately begin an inward battle: "I can't look. I have to 'bounce my eyes'; I have to 'protect my eye-gate.'" Before long your day at the mall basically stinks because you are fighting this inward battle the whole time. Eventually you just feel like: *I hate going to the mall* (or the beach or the gym or even church) *because of all these hot, tempting women.*

Option #2: While you notice that the mall is filled with beautiful women, you are also aware that you are a powerful, self-controlled, and valuable man of God. You do not choose option one, which would move you into an inward fight against temptation while your conscience condemns you. Instead, you are grieved in your heart that these ladies don't understand their value. (That is the heart of Jesus operating within you. If a beautiful woman understood her value, she wouldn't need to dress whorishly to try to gain value in the eyes of strangers.) Rather than spending your day fighting an inward battle, every time you see a beautiful woman, your heart responds, "Lord, thank You for creating such beauty. I ask that You would show my sister her inherent value and protect her from those who would steal that value from her. Amen." Once you fully grasp the truth of your identity, you will be able to relate to others according to their identity in God.

This renewing of the mind will not come in a moment. It must be put into practice, even daily, until you have altered your heart and mind, received a revelation, and are walking out a new identity. I have crafted a declaration that is used the same way that some individuals pray Psalm 91 or Psalm 23—as a way of renewing their minds to a specific truth. Here is the declaration that I use:

> *I declare freedom over every young woman trapped in the bonds of the sex industry. I pray for healing and restoration to your soul; that the shattered pieces of your heart would be put back together.*

Please forgive me for the times I have failed to protect and respect you; and especially for the times that I have directly dishonored you. I do not view you the way the world tells me to. You are beautiful, holy, and worthy of protecting. There is a perfect heavenly Father who wants you to feel His love, protection, and purity. And as your brother, I will always love, honor, and respect you.

Your beauty is meant for your family; therefore I appreciate what God has created, but I will not linger. I pray over my descendants that they will also view you in this way. I choose to operate in love and self-control; therefore I fix my eyes upon Jesus. He is my joy and my salvation. He will strengthen and renew my mind and spirit. He will be my comforter when I am sad, hurt, or lonely. I turn to Him!

THE LAST MILE

Since my readers are coming from a variety of experiences, it is a challenge to relate to each and every personal experience. However, no matter where you start in your journey from bondage to sexual purity, you will find that there are degrees of bondage that are left behind. For example, one reader may be struggling not to go to a strip club tonight; another may be struggling not to look at Internet porn; and yet another may be trying not to dwell on memories of an old flame. And while most Christian leaders teach against sexual impurity, they usually stop short of dealing with "the last mile."

A friend of mine described it this way:

The hardest part for me is what I call "the last mile"...where it's no longer about looking at porn or masturbating, but the little things that from the outside appear innocent, but in your heart you know the motives are not pure. Things like looking at a girl's Facebook profile just because she is hot. My wife could be in the same room and probably not notice, but the hidden motives behind that click are still the same as when it was pornographic images; it is still usury. It's so much easier to rationalize that click when it's seemingly innocent and you have excuses like "oh she is just an old friend from high school." But I don't want to give the enemy any foothold in my life, not even my pinky toenail.

The fact is that men will always notice beautiful women; God made those beautiful women and gave men the ability to visually appreciate that beauty. That alone is not sinful. The fact that you notice and appreciate beautiful women is not a bad thing. You have crossed the line into dangerous territory once you become *selfish* with what you are seeing.

As I stated earlier, men are destined by God to be protectors of beauty—whether in regard to nature, infants, art, health, or women. The influence of evolutionary thinking has caused many men to view themselves as animalistic in nature—that a man is simply nothing more than a highly evolved beast driven by sexual impulses.

Yet the Bible shows us that God created man to govern, cultivate, manage, protect, and expand the Garden of Eden. We need to realign our perspective to see that Adam was not put in The Garden to selfishly strip-mine the land of all of its inherent goodness. Adam was put on Earth as a protector, not as a predator. Predators steal, kill, and destroy beauty, whereas protectors value, appreciate, and respect beauty.

Imagine the following scenario with me. A man taught to be a beauty-predator is suddenly let loose in an art museum. He is overwhelmed by all the beauty that surrounds him, and because he has been bred a certain way, the only thing that he knows to do is to greedily snatch as many paintings as he can from the walls around him.

By contrast, a man who has been trained to be a protector (such as the museum security guard) will see the same beauty and acknowledge it. The difference is in the identities of the men: the predator is compelled to steal beauty for his selfish purposes, whereas the protector will appreciate the beauty, but leave it on the wall and protect it from predators.

When we see beauty, we must maintain our identity. We are not predators, but rather protectors of beauty. When we maintain our identity, we are able to see beautiful women as more than simply physical beings. We can appreciate the fact that they are people who need to be loved and protected to the core of their beings. Then we will value them as God values them.

This is how we run "the last mile."

Tool 1

Using the previous prayer example, craft a prayer of your own and carry it with you. Now put it to action. Tomorrow, place five pennies in your right pants pocket. Throughout the day, pray through your crafted prayer. Every time you pray it, move one penny to your left pocket. Your goal is to move all five pennies each day. Change frequency as needed.

If you find that you have been drawn back and tempted by the thought of a particular old girlfriend or a certain porn star or Hollywood actress, I suggest specifically targeting that person with your prayers. It is hard to know what spiritual connections have taken place through the past sins, but you are in the place now where you can release spiritual blessing and protection over your sisters everywhere. Now go for it!

Tool 2

When you encounter a beautiful woman, you must be prepared. It is time to stop being ashamed of the beauty that others carry. You will encounter beautiful women every day for the rest of your life, so just accept that fact and get over it. It is time to practice how to think when encountering beauty in a woman.

1. Acknowledge her beauty.

2. Take a moment and actually look at the beautiful woman.

3. Thank God for creating such beauty.

4. Ask the Lord for a deeper revelation about her being your sister.

5. Remind yourself that you are called as a protector.

6. Ponder what protecting her means and how you should view her.

7. Don't allow shame to wash over you; you are not a predator (don't listen to satan's lies).

8. Pray over her—that she would be protected, respected, and valued.

For practicality, over time I have whittled these eight steps down into one simple step. When I see a beautiful woman, I simply say in my heart, "I bless you in Jesus' name. Lord, I ask You to protect her and show her the inherent value she carries."

CHAPTER 12

SHE IS WORTH PROTECTING

We are not predators, we are protectors.

—JONATHAN WELTON

A strip club opened near my church in Chicago that was illegally allowing in minors. So I went to the owner of this strip club and confronted him about what he was allowing.

He responded, "Man, who are you anyway?"

I said, "I am Pastor Harvey Carey, the youth pastor of Salem Baptist church."

"Let me tell you something," he replied. "This is about the money, and what are you and a bunch of kids going to do about it anyway!"

So I went and got together with my youth group that night, which was about 900 students. My leadership and I dressed in our casual clothes so as to not look "churchy" and away we went. We lined up about 20 buses filled with students from our youth group. They parked around the corner from the strip club where they couldn't be seen.

My leadership and I approached the front door of the club and read the posted rules: "You must wear a shirt. You must wear shoes, and no hats allowed." Since we met the regulations we proceeded to enter the club.

I know some of you are thinking: "Oh my God pastor, that's not where Christians go!"

You idiot! Have you read the Bible! That is where Christians go! We go to change the world! Yes, light in darkness, not just light hanging out with light.

I called my leadership on the buses and said, "It is time!" The students poured off of the buses and surrounded the building on their knees in prayer.

[I] and the other youth group leaders with me inside the club approached the stage and bowed our knees in prayer. We began to cry out, "In the name of Jesus!"

Security approached us and said, "Sir, you cannot do that in here!"

I said, "Show me the sign! I am wearing a shirt. I am wearing shoes, and I don't have a hat on. I paid my $25 at the door and I can talk to God if I want to!"

The presence of God so filled that club as we prayed that the dancers were convicted and gathered up their belongings and left the building. All around the outside of the building, my youth group intercepted those precious former dancers and ministered to their hearts.

That night the club closed down and never reopened.[1]

I have made the point previously that men are called as rescuers and protectors of women. We are not predators; we are protectors. Here is a snapshot of the world's current situation. Reversing these numbers is our mission, our calling, our assignment:

- 1.4 million victims [women and children] are in servitude in the commercial sex industry.

- Less than 2 percent of these victims are rescued.

- One in 100,000 traffickers in Europe are convicted in court.[2]

- The U.N. reported in 2009 that up to 40 percent of women throughout Latin America have been victims of physical violence.

- In Asia, 60 million girls are "missing" due to prenatal sex selection, infanticide, or neglect. In China, young couples are allowed to have only one child, and boys are preferred. Baby girls are orphaned, thrown into rivers, left on doorsteps, or abandoned in forests.

- In many Islamic countries women die from *honor killings*. Women who dare to disagree with their husbands or show a hint of disrespect will be buried up to the waist by their husbands and other male relatives, and then stoned publically. This practice is illegal, yet it's estimated that thousands of such killings take place every year.

- Female genital mutilation affects an estimated 130 million women and girls, mostly in Africa. Each year, 2 million more undergo the barbaric practice.[3]

- "Author George Gilder in *Sexual Suicide* reported that men commit more than 90 percent of major crimes of violence, 100 percent of the rapes, and 95 percent of the burglaries. Men comprise 94 percent of our drunken drivers, 70 percent of suicides, 91 percent of offenders against family and children."[4]

Men, our sisters need us. They are literally crying out for our help. We cannot continue to play around with sin; we must become who God has called us to be and change what is happening in this world. Many of us want to see these atrocities end, and the first step is to get out of bondage to the evil spirits behind this industry. We must not allow our minds to view women the way that the devil tells us to. As former porn star turned Christian anti-porn activist, Shelley Lubben states in her book, our sisters need us!

> The real truth is we porn actresses want to end the shame and trauma of our box office lives but we can't do it alone. We need you men to fight for our freedom and give us back our honor. We need you to hold us in your strong arms while we sob tears over our deep wounds and begin to heal. We want you to throw out our movies and help piece together the shattered fragments of our lives. We need you to pray for us so God will hear and repair our ruined lives. Don't believe the big top fantasy. Porn is nothing more than fake sex, bruises and lies on video. Trust me, I know.[5]

It is time that we become like Christ. We have already discussed how we are called to treat women as our sisters, with dignity and respect. But being like Christ goes beyond not mistreating and lusting after our sisters. It is not enough to stop looking at them as objects of pleasure; it is time that we aggressively rise up and become rescuers, protectors, and Christlike heroes.

Most men who have struggled with sexual bondage continue to endure guilt and shame. They feel powerless and wonder if they will ever be free. If they have reached out for help from a therapist or read most of the current books on the subject, they are slapped with the label of *addict* and the promise, "once an addict, always an addict." Unfortunately, these men will continue to struggle from one methodology to another, looking only for their own freedom.

We must break out of this cycle. The millions of women who are being used, abused, and thrown away every day are crying out in their hearts, asking, "Will anyone ever truly love me and help me?"

God is not setting us free just so that we can be happy and not covered in shame. He does want us free, but for a purpose. We are freed to bring freedom to others. As Jesus said in Matthew 10:8, "... *Freely you have received; freely give.*"

You are either going to be a protector and rescuer, or you are going to be a user and abuser; there is no middle ground. Perhaps you have reasoned that you just look at a little bit of pornography and that you don't actually view and treat women as disposable objects of pleasure. Consider what you do when you are done viewing pornography. If you are like most men, you clear the history out of your computer's browser, you throw the magazine or DVD in the garbage, or you take the computer images and videos and place them into the trash can icon of your desktop.

Clearly you should remove this material from your life, yet the individual who downloads video clips each day and then throws them into the computer's trash can is implanting a powerful message into his brain: *Women can be used, abused, and thrown away. Women have no value and are completely disposable!*

We must become aggressive and stay on the offensive. If we become neutral or defensive in this fight, we will lose ground. As someone once said, "The reason that evil triumphs is because good men do nothing." Nobody is better prepared to respond to the evil atrocities occurring against women than the men who have been set free from this system of bondage. It is time for the 82 percent of Christian men who have been in captivity to get free, to rise up, and to bring freedom to women around the world.

Shouldn't the Church be leading the way in rescuing women caught in oppression? We have hidden our involvement in this sin long enough. It is time to own up, to get out of bondage, and to go back to rescue others.

Brother, wipe that shame off your face. You have a job to do. You may fall down a few more times while you are walking out of your life of bondage, but I have given you all of the tools to get free and stay free. The lynchpin to this whole issue is that you are not focused on your personal freedom as the end goal. You are getting free so that you can be like Christ and bring freedom to those who need it most. Once you are free from the grip of sexual bondage, don't leave your sisters imprisoned.

God is calling for spiritual warriors to rise up! We must hear the call and become prayer warriors and rescuers. Our sisters and daughters need us; it is time for men to rise to the rescue!

Tool

Get a men's group at your church to read through this book. You are not meeting to struggle for personal freedom together. You are coming together as a rescue squad. Pray the crafted prayer together and ask the Lord to give you wisdom and insight regarding how you can reach out to the women trapped in a sexual-bondage lifestyle. Here are a few ideas:

1.   Meet across the street from a strip club and pray for those women to come to know the perfect love of their heavenly Father.

2.   Write to a porn star telling him/her of the true freedom and shame-free life they can have in Christ. Tell him/her how God loves and yearns for them.

3. Write to ministries that are working with women in the sex slave trade and encourage them in their mission. Their work is lonely, and your support will bless them tremendously.

4. Visit the street(s) in your city where prostitution takes place. Hit the streets two by two and give out roses to the women you meet. Share with them how God sees them as His rose and how He loves them.

5. Have a men's breakfast periodically to encourage men to rise up, not only for personal freedom, but also as the heroes that women need in this world.

CHAPTER 13

She Needs Love

God hates sluts, whores, and home-wreckers!
—A STREET PREACHER
misrepresenting Christ's love

For many years, the Church has struggled in its approach to evangelizing the world. We know that we are not to love the world system. Too often, we have forgotten that we are also called to love those who are caught in the world system. We have been quick to become like the Pharisees who brought the woman caught in adultery to Jesus, hoping to incite a public stoning (see John 8:2-11). We are so indignant about the sin that we become hateful toward those caught in the trap of sin. But this absolutely does not reflect the heart of God toward those living sinful lifestyles.

In this chapter I am presenting a challenge to love those who are caught in promiscuous lifestyles. If we are going to follow Jesus' example, then prostitutes should feel loved by us and want to be around us. After all, they flocked to be around Jesus, and He was called a "friend of sinners" (see Luke 7:34). Jesus said that we must likewise love our enemies (see Matt. 5:44). Yet strippers, porn stars, and prostitutes do not feel loved by the Church (and they aren't even our enemies).

Most individuals in the sex industry will never step foot inside a church because they fear our rejection or judgment. In addition, they feel dirty, and the concept of church that they've learned from us is not that of a safe place for those dirtied with sin. Unfortunately, the typical Christian response to this is, "Of course they don't feel comfortable in church. They are sinners, and they are being convicted!"

Yet, those who hung around Jesus didn't feel condemned, dirty, rejected, or judged. Rather, many of them felt so loved and honored that they responded like Mary Magdalene (see Mark 16:9-10) and Zaccheus (see Luke 19:1-10), who were compelled by love to turn from their sins and find freedom in Jesus. Consider the immoral woman who felt so loved by Jesus and so safe with Him that she risked the scorn of the Pharisees in order to demonstrate her gratitude by anointing Jesus with her tears (see Luke 7:36-50). If we are going to be like Jesus, sinners should never feel judged or rejected or dirty around us.

No More Picketing

My friend Anny Donewald is a former stripper and prostitute who came to know Jesus and was set free from all her bondage. She now runs a ministry that reaches out to girls who are still working in the industry. Recently, she helped bring resolution to a conflict in Ohio between a church and a local strip club. The pastor of the church clearly did not understand the heart of Jesus and decided to picket against the strip club every weekend; his church did this for four years! Eventually, the dancers from the club decided to retaliate by picketing the church! The conflict escalated to the point of making the national news. That was when Anny Donewald got involved, but I will let her tell you the rest of the story in her own words:

It was a Tuesday when it all started. I was headed to my regular Tuesday Bible study/outreach in Grand Rapids, Michigan and had a question for the pastor of the church where we hold our meetings. I went into his office a little before we started, and said, "Hey. I think the Lord is telling me that we're about to hit the press. I think we should do a press release on this ministry. How do I do that?"

He gave me the direction on how to do it and then said, "Hey Anny, before you go, have you heard of this story in Ohio? The church has been picketing a strip club for years, and now the strip club is picketing the church!"

I quickly replied, "Nope! Haven't heard of it. That's too bad. I'll make sure I pray for that situation." I left his office, and didn't think twice about that story.

The next day was a Wednesday, and I had to take my sister-in-law to the airport in Chicago. The whole way there, my spirit was very excited. It felt like something was up, and I couldn't figure out what. The excitement did not go away, but intensified, and after I dropped off my sister-in-law and turned around to come home, I started to pray. At this point, it was almost uncomfortable, and I realized the Lord was saying something. I said out loud, "God. What are You saying? I can't understand! Send someone to call me, because I can't quite get what it is that You're trying to tell me."

No sooner did five minutes pass and the phone rang. My friend, Sheri Brown, from San Diego, California, was on the other line, and the first thing she said to me was, "Hey girl. Did you read this story about what's going on in Ohio?"

Immediately, I knew. I knew God was telling me to go do reconciliation with the club and the church. After I explained my "Ah hah" moment, Sheri said she wanted to come with me. So, as I drove back to Michigan from Chicago, Illinois, we planned. By the time I got home, it was less than 48 hours until we arrived in Columbus, Ohio.

Sheri and I got to the hotel within 15 minutes of each other. Immediately, we started praying over the gift bags we'd made for the girls, and I started to prophetically write on cards a Word of God for each one of the girls. We prayed that each Word would be specific to the girls and their situations; whatever they were going through, God knew. Instead of waiting until Saturday night to take the girls their gifts, we got dressed, got ready, and off we went to the strip club, which was named The Foxhole.

When we got there, people were outside—including police and picketers; we walked right past them into the club. We weren't sure how they were going to receive us because we were coming as Christians, but I met the main girl at the door and told her who we were. She was very happy to meet us and invited us right into the dressing room. We were in there for about two hours, explaining to them that we both had ministries, that I used to be a dancer and a prostitute, that God wasn't picketing, that Jesus loves them, and that God told me to come specifically and rectify the situation. They loved us! And they loved their gifts. We told them that we'd come back the next day and bring pizza.

The next day, we got up, got ready, sent out e-mails, called our families back home, went out to eat, and set out again for The Foxhole. There was a Little Caesar's somewhere close to the club, and we stopped and got five pizzas. I knew I'd heard the Lord say, "Get one for the picketing Christians." They were the last people I wanted to talk to. I was disgusted with their disgust. But, I was obedient and bought the church picketers a pizza.

We spent a few hours in the dressing room again. The Holy Spirit was all over the place. The prophetic was moving strongly on me, and I was able to give them words of knowledge about things that there would be no natural explanation as to how I would know. It removed the myth that God was mad at them, because clearly, He'd shown up in their dressing room. We prayed and fellowshipped about the truth of the Gospel, and then we ate pizza. Finally, when it was time to leave, I was so under the anointing that I saw the church people outside the club and hugged them and gave them their pizza too.

I was able to share my testimony with the men who were picketing and told them that it wasn't the wrath of people, but the love of God, that transformed my life. I told them that the women in the club did not feel that love coming from them; their actions were making them feel defensive. They listened, we prayed, and then they invited us to speak at their church the next morning. Can you believe that?

We went back to the hotel room. I slept two hours, and Sheri didn't sleep at all. We woke up, got ready early, and set out for a church called (of all things) New Beginnings. We were a bit early, and the press was outside the church ready to do their usual story. Soon, the girls from The Foxhole showed up to picket in their bikinis. We hugged, I invited them in; they said they didn't feel welcome, and I told them I'd be out in a minute.

After sharing my story and Sheri explaining what she and Theresa Scher do (her co-leader of JC's Girls in San Diego), the church service concluded. Low and behold, as we walked outside, church people were hugging strippers, and strippers were hugging church people. The press was taking pictures, and Sheri and I were standing on the steps of that church with our jaws on the floor. We couldn't believe what we were seeing. Mission accomplished. Or so it seemed.

Since then, the pastor of New Beginnings decided that it would be a good idea to continue to picket. I have not spoken to the pastor since we left that Sunday afternoon. It saddens me that this was his decision, but I've chosen to leave that between him and God. I was obedient to what the Lord said, and to this day, I am still in contact with the girls at The Foxhole. I still pray for them, and they still pray for me!

How were the girls affected? Out of six strippers, three re-dedicated their lives to the Lord, two made salvation decisions, and one is considering her future.

A More Excellent Way

The Church has always wanted to reach people for Christ, but some of the methods that we have employed have been absolutely harmful. Although I believe in power evangelism, friendship evangelism, presence evangelism, and servant evangelism, we need to return to the essence of the Gospel—love. Too often we have tried to address the problems of immorality by politically or socially attacking the sin (and sometimes the sinner)—as with the picketers in Anny's story—rather than focusing our efforts on loving the sinners out of their sins. This does not mean trying to change them, but simply loving them with God's love and trusting Him to free them. When we require others to change in order for them to receive our love, we are not conveying the heart of God.

Ironically, this attitude of self-righteous judgment, because it is not righteousness, often opens the door to sin in our own lives. Thus, as I mentioned previously, many believers outwardly condemn the sin while inwardly struggling with it. If we would learn to "fight" with love and compassion, prostitutes would be more likely to get saved, and Christians would be less likely to struggle with sexual sin.

It is time that we lay down our methods and listen to the apostle Paul, who said, *"And yet I will show you a more excellent way"* (1 Cor. 12:31). He followed this statement by laying out an incredible description of the God-kind of love:

> *If I speak in the tongues of men or of angels, but do not have love, I am only a resounding gong or a clanging cymbal. If I have the gift of prophecy and can fathom all mysteries and all knowledge, and if I have a faith that can move mountains, but do not have love, I am nothing. If I give all I possess to the poor and give over my body to hardship that I may boast, but do not have love, I gain nothing.*
>
> *Love is patient, love is kind. It does not envy, it does not boast, it is not proud. It does not dishonor others, it is not self-seeking, it is not easily angered, it keeps no record of wrongs. Love does not delight in evil but rejoices with the truth. It always protects, always trusts, always hopes, always perseveres* (1 Corinthians 13:1-7).

On Christmas Eve of 2005, I had an idea. I purchased ten brand-new hooded sweaters, winter hats, gloves, and scarves. (Rochester, New York, has cold winters.) I put them into neat piles, each with a bow on top, and my friend Mark and I drove down to the area known for prostitutes' streetwalking.

Mark was my driver and lookout. We drove up and down the street, and each time we found a girl, we parked a block away. Then I would grab one of my piles (sweater, hat, gloves, and a scarf) with a bow on top and walk briskly to the girl before she came to our car. We must have been quite a sight at first because, at the time, I was 22 years old, and the typical customer would have stayed in his car.

Upon meeting each of these startled girls, I would share with them that God had sent me to them to give them their Christmas present. Then I would hug them and pray for them. Without fail, every single girl cried and was touched deeply that night.

One girl I remember in particular. It was the end of the night, it was incredibly cold, and I had run out of gift piles. Mark and I were about to head home when I noticed the youngest girl we had seen all night; she was perhaps in her late teens, compared to most of the girls who were in their 30s or 40s. I hadn't seen her before, but I saw that she had a brand-new hat on; it still had the tag hanging off, and it was one of our hats!

We pulled over and she yelled to me, "You must be Jonathan!"

A little startled, I asked her where she got the hat. She said that Donna had given it to her. (Donna was the last girl we had talked and prayed with.) Donna had also told her that the hat was from God and that He loved her and wanted her to have a wonderful Christmas. (Apparently, Donna was now a regional evangelist in the area. I am only half-joking.)

The young girl's name was Ashley. I said to her, "You look really cold. I am sorry, but we have run out of sweaters."

"Yeah, I am cold," she said, "but you have already blessed me so much."

Thinking quickly, I decided to take off my own coat. "Ashley, Jesus loves you so much. I can't leave without giving you this."

As I wrapped my coat around her, Ashley looked me in the eye as if she hadn't ever received an act of love in her whole life. "Jonathan...is that what God is like?"

"Yeah, Ashley, that is what He is like."

With tears pouring from both our eyes, we embraced, and I prayed everything I could think of over this daughter of the King. No, she didn't change the course of her life that night, but seeds of love were planted in her heart.

A year later, Mark and I hit the street again to give out Christmas presents. This time we also brought teddy bears with us because many of these girls have children at home and wouldn't be able to get them Christmas presents.

The best part of our second-year trip was when we pulled over and a girl came running to our car. She said, "Jonathan! I thought it was you. I had the feeling that it was you when you pulled up!"

"Ashley, is that you?"

It was! She continued in her lifestyle, but love had made a lasting impression upon her life. God came down and touched her, and she hadn't forgotten. Love is the seed we must plant if we desire to have lasting fruit. Ashley needs more love. Like anyone who has gotten caught in the sex industry; she has come from a long road of brokenness.

A HISTORY OF PAIN

"According to former porn actress, April Garris, a counselor to ex porn stars: 'In most every single case, there is some background of childhood sexual abuse or neglect.'"[1] The recent documentary film, *Very Young Girls,* stated that the average age of when girls enter into a life of prostitution is 13 years old.[2]

Most shocking was when Anny Donewald told me of this survey finding: "The vast majority [of exotic dancers] (89 percent) were raised in a religious home."[3] These are church girls who have been wounded, hurt, and damaged. Statistics further show that most children are abused by someone they know and love, often a member of their extended family.[4] The majority of these hurting women grew up in environments that should have shown them the meaning of true, pure love. Considering that one out of every six women in the U.S. is at some point in her life the victim of an attempted or completed rape,[5] it is not hard to conclude that our world is filled with many hurting women.

Much of the reason why women end up in the sex industry is because of a love deficit in their lives. Whether from abuse or neglect, our sisters are hurting. They desperately need love, and Jesus' followers are supposed to be known by their love! (See John 13:35.) It is time for us to remove our judgments and to make sure that our wounded sisters feel the love of Christ flowing through us. I would like to propose a plan of action.

ADOPT-A-STRIP-CLUB!

Currently there are 3,829 adult cabarets nationwide in America.[6] Also there are approximately 500,000 churches in America.[7] What if we, the Church, as the representatives of Jesus in the Earth, actively began to love the hurting sisters in our communities?

I am proposing the Adopt-A-Strip-Club program. In this program, each church in America would find the nearest strip club and regularly pray for the redemption of the club's workers and patrons. If all 500,000 churches in America took this idea seriously, there would be 130 churches praying for each strip club in America!

It is time for both Christian men and women in every community to communicate to the women caught in the sex industry that they are loved. The Body of Christ needs to tell those involved in the sex industry that they are not too dirty to come to church. Instead, we must let them know that, should they want to come to church, they would be loved and accepted, not judged and rejected. We must make our love known; we must not hide our light under a basket!

Tool

I am currently working with Anny Donewald to expand the Adopt-A-Strip-Club program. If you would like help in training your people, bridging the gap between your church and the local club, and reaching your local club for Christ, please contact Anny Donewald through www.Evesangels.org.

SECTION 3 SUMMARY

All women are our sisters. We are to view them as family, not objects to be used for selfish pleasure. Yes, they are beautiful and lovely; and as men, we will notice them for the rest of our lives; but there is a way to appreciate without defiling.

Evolution has taught us that man evolved as a predator; the truth is that God created men as protectors of beauty. This aspect of our identity must shift so that we can understand our role in relation to women.

Most women in the sex industry worldwide are victims of sexual, emotional, verbal, and physical abuse. They know no lifestyle outside of fear and abuse; yet in their hearts they long for a protector to come to their defense. Will we remain cowards behind a computer screen, using our sisters for selfish purposes? Or will we fight for their freedom?

Epilogue

How does it feel, knowing you can be completely free from the temptation and sexual sin that haunted you? How does it feel to no longer think of yourself as a hopeless victim, but to know your true identity as a son of God? If you've visited or camped in the despair that so often plagues Christian men who struggle with these issues, I imagine you feel a sense of exhilaration as you breathe in these truths from God's Word.

You are powerful and you are valuable. No more victim mentality or blame-shifting for you. And no more hiding in fear of others either, trying to fill your intimacy hole by selling your freedom to addictions. Rather, you now see that you are a self-controlled man who can communicate assertively and establish healthy boundaries. You are settling in to the reality of how God sees you—not according to your past, but according to your future. After all, that old nature and your propensity to sin have been crucified once and for all with Jesus. Now you are the righteousness of Christ and as a new creation, you are empowered by His grace to live without sin. For you, there will be no more striving and trying to "die daily" to your flesh, only resting in the accomplished work of Christ.

You have a new perspective on your adversary, too. After all, you know now that you're in the victory chariot with Jesus, and satan's dragging behind you in humiliation. Triumph feels good, and you plan on living there the rest of your life. You know you can't live in victory through your own effort—now you see why the law was written in the first place (to show you your need for Jesus). Rather than focusing on all those *don'ts,* you lean into the New Covenant's *but rathers.* You turn your places of pain into places of prayer and send the devil fleeing. When temptation comes, you recognize it as promotion because you know the Father has prepared you to succeed. Equipped with your revelation of your identity in Him, you quickly respond as a powerful man. To the accusations of shame, you apply the blood of Jesus, which cleanses your conscience every time. Hearing the Holy Spirit's conviction of sin, you repent, and then you listen to hear His statements about your righteousness and His commission to enact judgment on the enemy. And you forgive until the pain is gone.

You know this isn't just about you. Freedom's purpose is much bigger than one man. So you give freedom away by loving women. Now you see them as they truly are—daughters of God, your sisters and mothers—and so you love them purely. Women are not the problem and neither is their beauty. Rather, it is part of your purpose as a man to protect women and their beauty, praying that all women would know how their Papa sees them. When you see a woman who is dressed scantily or who is part of the sex industry, you now see her according to God's heart. You grieve for her brokenness and pain, and you proactively do what you can to show her God's love.

You are a true man.

ENDNOTES

INTRODUCTION

1. Watchman Nee, *The Life That Wins* (New York: Christian Fellowship Publishers, 1986), 7.

2. Mark Driscoll, *Porn-Again Christian* (Seattle, Washington: Mars Hill Church, 2011), 28.

3. Watchman Nee, *The Life That Wins*, 32-33.

CHAPTER 1: MY STORY

1. "In his book, *The Sexual Man*, Dr. Archibald Hart revealed the results of a survey of some 600 Christian men on the topic of masturbation: 61% of married Christian men masturbate; 82% of these have self sex on an average of once a week; 10% have sex with self 5-10 times per month, 6% more than 15 times per month, and 1% more than 20 times a month. [Thirteen percent] of Christian married men said they felt it was normal." Passage quoted from: Mike Genung, "Statistics and information on pornography in the USA," *Blazing Grace*, 2005, http://www.blazinggrace.org/cms/bg/pornstats (accessed March 14, 2011).

2. "SeXXX Business Statistics," *Cross Cultural Connections*, http://crossculturalconnections.org/documents/sex_stats.pdf (accessed March 14, 2011).

3. "Pastors and Adultery," *Gay Christian Movement Watch*, http://www.gcmwatch.com/4752/pastors-and-adultery (accessed March 14, 2011).

4. Thomas F. Fischer, "The Affair-Proof Pastorate," http://www.ministryhealth.net/mh_articles/294_affair_proof_pastorate.html (accessed March 14, 2011).

5.	For more on deliverance, I highly recommend reading *Victory Over the Darkness* by Neil T. Anderson.

6.	I have found Wellspring Ministries in Anchorage, Alaska to be a tremendous ministry for inner healing.

CHAPTER 2: YOU ARE POWERFUL

1.	"The Twelve Steps," Sex Addicts Anonymous, http://saa-recovery.org/OurProgram/TheTwelveSteps/ (accessed December 29, 2011).

2.	Blue Letter Bible, "Dictionary and Word Search for Midyan (Strong's 4080)," Blue Letter Bible (1996-2011) http://www.blueletterbible.org/lang/lexicon/lexicon.cfm?Strongs=H4080&t=KJV <http://www.blueletterbible.org/lang/lexicon/lexicon.cfm?Strongs=H4080&t=KJV> (accessed December 29, 2011).

3.	Danny Silk, *Loving Our Kids on Purpose* (Shippensburg, PA: Destiny Image, 2008), 46.

4.	"Corrie Ten Boom Story on Forgiving," Family Life Education Institute, http://www.familylifeeducation.org/gilliland/procgroup/CorrieTenBoom.htm, (accessed July 26, 2011).

5.	*Rocky Balboa*, screenplay by Sylvester Stallone; film produced by Metro-Goldwyn-Mayer, Columbia Pictures, Revolution Studios, and Rogue Marble, released in 2006.

6.	Uri Paz, "Victor Frankl's Forgiveness," http://www.mediate.com/articles/omedia1.cfm, (accessed July 26, 2011).

7.	Danny Silk, "Communication Dance," *Defining the Relationship* (DVD); available at http://www.dtr.lovingonpurpose.com/.

8.	There are certain connections that we must be protected from. We will discuss that in the next chapter in the section on Healthy Boundaries.

9.	*Vine's Expository Dictionary of Biblical Words*, (Thomas Nelson Publishers, 1985), s.v. "sumphoneo" (NT 4857).

10.	Merriam-Webster Online, *Merriam-Webster Online Dictionary 2011*, s.v. "symphony," http://www.merriam-webster.com/dictionary/symphony (accessed December 29, 2011).

CHAPTER 3: YOU ARE VALUABLE

1.	Ryan Blue, "Saving Private Ryan—The Value of 1 Person Compared to 8," movie review, *Faith and Film: Mosaic Movie Connect Group* (February 22, 2008); http://mosaicmovieconnectgroup.blogspot.com/2008/02/saving-private-ryan-value-of-1-person.html (accessed July 26, 2011).

2.	Danny Silk, *Loving Our Kids on Purpose* (Shippensburg, PA: Destiny Image, 2008), 93.

3. For more about knowing God's secrets read the chapter entitled, "Entrusted With Secrets," from my book, *The School of the Seers* (Shippensburg, PA: Destiny Image Publishers, 2009).

CHAPTER 4: YOU ARE NOT YOUR ACTIONS

1. Neil T. Anderson and Robert L. Saucy, *The Common Made Holy* (Eugene, OR: Harvest House Publishers, 1997), 87.

2. *Rocky Balboa*, screenplay by Sylvester Stallone; film produced by Metro-Goldwyn-Mayer, Columbia Pictures, Revolution Studios, and Rogue Marble, released in 2006.

3. Danny Silk, *Culture of Honor* (Shippensburg, PA: Destiny Image, 2009), 173.

CHAPTER 5: YOU ARE CRUCIFIED IN CHRIST

1. Charles Dickens, *David Copperfield* (New York: Random House, 2000), 123 (emphasis added).

2. Author's note: Theologian Gordon Fee affirms this point of view by pointing out that the Holy Spirit is not mentioned in the inner struggle explained in Romans 7:14-24. Regarding Gordon Fee's input, see page 22-23 of *Power, Holiness, and Evangelism*, compiled by Randy Clark.

3. Author's note: I have been asked many times about Romans 8:1 which says in the King James Version: *"There is therefore now no condemnation to them which are in Christ Jesus, who walk not after the flesh, but after the Spirit."* This verse seems to state that there are two classes of Christians, those who walk after the flesh, which are condemned and those who walk after the Spirit and are not condemned.

   Unfortunately, this verse has been mistranslated from the original manuscripts. A simple check of any Interlinear Greek/English Bible (for example: http://biblos.com/romans/8-1.htm; or Karl Ellinger and Wilhelm Rudolph, Adrian Schenker eds., *Interlinear Transliterated Bible, Fifth Revised Edition*, (Biblesoft Inc., 1994, 2003, 2006).) These show that the original manuscripts only say, *"There is therefore now no condemnation to them which are in Christ Jesus."* There are not two classes of Christian; the KJV translators added to this verse, whereas most modern translations remove the second half of the sentence because it has no basis in the original manuscript.

4. B.A. Robinson, "Glossary of Religious and Spiritual Terms," Religious Tolerance, May 20, 2007, http://www.religioustolerance.org/gl_j.htm (accessed August 19, 2011).

5. Thayer and Smith, *New Testament Greek Lexicon*, Study Light, s.v. "Enduo"; http://www.studylight.org/lex/grk/view.cgi?number=1746 (accessed March 14, 2011).

CHAPTER 6: YOU ARE A NEW CREATION

1. For more information about meditation on God's Word, see the "Biblical Meditation" chapter in *School of the Seers* (Shippensburg, PA: Destiny Image Publishers, 2009).

CHAPTER 8: THE LAW

1. For more information about legalism and how to be free of it, read the chapter, "A Slave of Freedom" from my book, *Normal Christianity* (Shippensburg, PA: Destiny Image, 2011).

CHAPTER 9: TEMPTATION

1. Kenneth Wuest comments that *peirazo* "referred first to the action of putting someone to the test to see what good or evil is in the one tested, and second, because so many broke down under the test and committed sin, the word came to mean a 'solicitation to do evil.' Both meanings are in view here. Our Lord in His incarnation as the Last Adam, was put to the test and was also solicited to do evil (Mt 4:1-11 *'Then Jesus was led up by the Spirit into the wilderness to be tempted by the devil.'*)" Kenneth Wuest, *Wuest's Word Studies from the Greek New Testament* (Grand Rapids, MI: Eerdmans, 1980).

    "Whether the tests become a proof of righteousness or an inducement to evil depends on our response. If we resist in God's power, the tests becomes a test that proves our faithfulness. If we do not resist in His power (or try to resist in our own power), the test becomes a solicitation to sin. The Bible uses *peirazo* in both ways." Quoted from: Precept Austin, "Hebrews 2:18," http://www.preceptaustin.org/hebrews_218.htm (accessed May 8, 2011).

2. *Vine's Expository Dictionary of New Testament Words*, (Thomas Nelson, 1985) s.v. "tempt."

3. The phrase *against sin* indicates that sin is "personified as an adversary." *The Jamieson-Fausset-Brown Bible Commentary*; Hebrews 12:4; as quoted by Biblios, http://biblecommenter.com/hebrews/12-4.htm (accessed May 8, 2011).

4. *'Ye have not yet resisted unto blood, striving against sin.'* The general sense of this passage is, 'you have not yet been called in your Christian struggles to the highest kind of sufferings and sacrifices. Great as your trials may seem to have been, yet your faith has not yet been put to the severest test. And since this is so, you ought not to yield in the conflict with evil, but manfully resist it.' In the language

used here, there is undoubtedly a continuance of the allusion to the agonistic games—the strugglings and wrestlings for mastery there. In those games, the boxers were accustomed to arm themselves for the fight with the caestus. This at first consisted of strong leathern thongs wound around the hands, and extending only to the wrist, to give greater solidity to the fist. Afterward these were made to extend to the elbow, and then to the shoulder, and finally, they sewed pieces of lead or iron in them that they might strike a heavier and more destructive blow. The consequence was, that those who were engaged in the fight were often covered with blood, and that resistance "unto blood" showed a determined courage, and a purpose not to yield. But though the language here may be taken from this custom, the fact to which the apostle alludes, it seems to me, is the struggling of the Saviour in the Garden of Gethsemane, when his conflict was so severe that, great drops of blood fell down to the ground[—]see the notes on Matthew 26:36-44. It is, indeed, commonly understood to mean that they had not yet been called to shed their blood as martyrs in the cause of religion...." Quoted from Biblios, http://biblecommenter.com/hebrews/12-4.htm (accessed May 8, 2011).

CHAPTER 10: SHAME

1. It is important to state that I am not teaching Universalism, which claims that God will eventually bring to Heaven those who are in hell. While all sin has been forgiven, hell will be filled with those who chose to reject forgiveness rather than receive forgiveness by faith and repentance. Forgiveness is a gift, and many people choose not to receive this gift.

2. Merriam-Webster Online, *Merriam-Webster Online Dictionary 2011*, s.v. "condemn," http://www.merriam-webster.com/dictionary/condemn (accessed December 30, 2011).

3. Ibid.

4. Ibid., s.v. "conviction," http://www.merriam-webster.com/dictionary/conviction (accessed December 30, 2011).

CHAPTER 11: SHE IS YOUR SISTER

1. Neil Anderson, *Victory Over the Darkness* (Ventura, CA: Regal, 2000), 42.

CHAPTER 12: SHE IS WORTH PROTECTING

1. Pastor Harvey Carey shared this at Niagara Conference 2003.

2. *Charisma Magazine* (December 2010), 60.

3. Ibid., 50.

4. Stephen Arterburn, Fred Stoeker, and Mike Yorkey, *Every Man's Battle* (Colorado Springs, CO: WaterBrook Press, 2000), 62.

5. Shelley Lubben, *Truth Behind the Fantasy of Porn: The Greatest Illusion on Earth* (Shelley Lubben Communications, 2010), 7.

CHAPTER 13: SHE NEEDS LOVE

1. Shelley Lubben, *Truth Behind the Fantasy of Porn: The Greatest Illusion on Earth* (Shelley Lubben Communications, 2010), 10, quoting April Garris, "Myth 2 Exposed," The Porn Effect Blog, http://www.whodoesithurt.com/april-garris/177-april-garris.

2. *Very Young Girls*, directed by David Shisgall and Nina Alvarez, produced by Swinging T Productions, 2007.

3. Constance Bernard et al., (Old Dominion University Department of Sociology and Criminal Justice), "Exotic Dancers: Gender Differences in Societal Reaction, Subcultural Ties, and Conventional Support," http://www.albany.edu/scj/jcjpc/vol10is1/bernard.pdf (accessed April 18, 2011).

4. Susan K. Flinn, "Child Sexual Abuse I: An Overview," Advocates for Youth, January, 1995, http://www.advocatesforyouth.org/index.php?option=com_content&task=view&id=410&Itemid=336 (accessed July 27, 2011).

5. "Who Are the Victims?" Rape, Abuse, & Incest National Network, http://www.rainn.org/get-information/statistics/sexual-assault-victims (accessed July 27, 2011).

6. "SeXXX Business Statistics," Cross Cultural Connections, http://crossculturalconnections.org/documents/sex_stats.pdf (accessed March 27, 2011).

7. Jonathan Welton, *Normal Christianity* (Shippensburg, PA: Destiny Image, 2011), 12.

About Jonathan Welton

A fifth generation believer, Jonathan Welton is propelled by a powerful Christian heritage. As a Kingdom theologian, Jonathan raises the standard for walking in wisdom, character, and power. Even those who have grown up in the church are challenged afresh as they hear the unique perspective that Jonathan carries.

Jonathan has earned two Master's degrees, one in Biblical Studies and the other in Practical Ministry, as well as the National Herald of Christ award. He is currently working on his Doctorate in Theology.

Jonathan is the best-selling author of *The School of the Seers, Normal Christianity, and Raptureless*. He and his wife, Karen, live in Rochester, New York.

For more information about Jonathan Welton's ministry see
www.WeltonAcademy.com

IN THE RIGHT HANDS, THIS BOOK WILL CHANGE LIVES!

Most of the people who need this message will not be looking for this book. To change their lives, you need to put a copy of this book in their hands.

> *But others (seeds) fell into good ground, and brought forth fruit, some a hundred-fold, some sixty-fold, some thirty-fold* (Matthew 13:8).

Our ministry is constantly seeking methods to find the good ground, the people who need this anointed message to change their lives. Will you help us reach these people?

> *Remember this—a farmer who plants only a few seeds will get a small crop. But the one who plants generously will get a generous crop* (2 Corinthians 9:6).

EXTEND THIS MINISTRY BY SOWING
3 BOOKS, 5 BOOKS, 10 BOOKS, **OR MORE TODAY,**
AND BECOME A LIFE CHANGER!

Thank you,

Don Nori Sr., Founder
Destiny Image
Since 1982

DESTINY IMAGE PUBLISHERS, INC.

"Promoting Inspired Lives."

VISIT OUR NEW SITE HOME AT
WWW.DESTINYIMAGE.COM

FREE SUBSCRIPTION TO DI NEWSLETTER

Receive free unpublished articles by top DI authors, exclusive
discounts, and free downloads from our best and newest books.
Visit www.destinyimage.com to subscribe.

Write to: Destiny Image
                P.O. Box 310
                Shippensburg, PA 17257-0310

Call: 1-800-722-6774

Email: orders@destinyimage.com

For a complete list of our titles or to place an order
online, visit www.destinyimage.com.